11 ⁵⁰

Fifty
FAMOUS AMERICANS

Fifty
FAMOUS AMERICANS

★ ★ ★ ★ ★ ★ ★ ★ ★ ★ ★

By
WARD GRIFFITH

Illustrated by
HENRY E. VALLELY

Biography Index Reprint Series

BOOKS FOR LIBRARIES PRESS
FREEPORT, NEW YORK

STANDARD BOOK NUMBER:

8369-8017-4

LIBRARY OF CONGRESS CATALOG CARD NUMBER:

79-117325

PRINTED IN THE UNITED STATES OF AMERICA

CONTENTS

CONTENTS *(Continued)*

CONTENTS *(Continued)*

Orville and Wilbur Wright

Men With Wings

EVER SINCE the world began boys and girls, and men and women, too, have been saying, "I wish I could fly!" By inventing the airplane, Wilbur and Orville Wright made that wish come true. They gave men wings and made neighbors of all the peoples of the world.

Today it is possible to have dinner one evening in San Francisco and lunch the next day in New York City. One can leave New York one day and be in Ireland the next. The Wright brothers' invention did for transportation what the invention of the telegraph did for communication.

Wilbur Wright was born April 16, 1867, near Millville, Indiana. Shortly after his birth, the family moved to Dayton, Ohio, where Orville was born August 19, 1871. There the boys grew up.

Orville and Wilbur inherited their inventive skill from their mother, a capable and ingenious woman with a knack for contriving gadgets. One year she built a bobsled for the boys'

11

Christmas.

Their father, Milton Wright, was a bishop of the Church of United Brethren in Christ. One day Bishop Wright brought the boys a toy which interested them more than any they had ever seen. It was a helicopter—a miniature bamboo airplane with cardboard propellers. The propellers turned by means of twisted rubber bands and carried the little flying machine gracefully through the air.

Wilbur and Orville were delighted. Dubbing their new toy a bat, they flew it till it fell apart. After that they built many bats of their own, thereby learning their first lesson in aeronautics.

After finishing high school, the two young men started a small bicycle factory. In 1896, Wilbur read of the death of Otto Lilienthal and of his unsuccessful experiments with gliding machines. Wilbur was greatly impressed. He showed the stories to Orville and from that day on, the two had one ambition—to succeed where Lilienthal had failed.

They read everything they could find on the subject of aeronautics. They studied air currents, air pressure and wind velocity.

They experimented with kites, making a biplane kite with wings that could be moved forward and back and could be moved in a twisting or warping motion. In this way they were able to regulate the balance of the kite. They also used an elevator at the back of the first kite, much the same way that the rear elevator on a plane is used today. They learned from their kite flying that their theories about the maintenance of equilibrium were workable and they continued to try to perfect their ideas.

After a great deal of experimenting, they decided to make a man-carrying glider and to fly it as a kite to get practice in operating it. In a few weeks they had built their glider of bent wood ribs covered with cloth.

The next problem was to find a place to test their giant bird. Who could tell them where the winds were strongest and steadiest? The United States Weather Bureau, of course! After studying the information they received from the government, they decided that Kitty Hawk, North Carolina, would be the best place for their testing ground.

There, in October, 1900, the glider was flown like a kite, and piloted from below by means of ropes. No man was aboard, but the glider carried about fifty pounds of chain. The balancing system was operated by cords from the ground. Their kite-glider was a success and showed them they were on the right track.

Later that same year, they tried gliding down a large sand dune known as Kill Devil Hill. In making these glides, the machine was never more than two or three feet from the ground, but the brothers had a chance to try out their balancing mechanism in actual flight.

The following year they returned to Kitty Hawk and continued their experiments, but it was not until 1903 that they were ready to add propellers and a motor to their biplane.

The general public paid little attention to the experiments of the Wright brothers. Indeed, little publicity was given them. People looked upon them as just another pair of men trying to realize the dream of flying, and for centuries men had tried but had never succeeded.

When the announcement was made that the brothers would test their first motor-driven plane on December 17, 1903, at Kitty Hawk, only five people bothered to go to the hillside. Those five never forgot the day.

It was Orville's turn to try the plane. Climbing into it he became the first person to successfully fly a motor-powered airplane. His flight lasted only twelve seconds it is true, but those twelve seconds made history. Later Wilbur flew eight hundred fifty-two feet, staying up fifty-nine seconds.

Two years later, with a greatly improved plane, the Wrights made a flight of a little more than twenty-four miles.

They had now proved that their invention was practical. The problem now was what to do with it. A decision was quickly reached: they would offer their plane to the government.

They wrote to their congressman, offering to provide machines of agreed specifications or to furnish the government with scientific and practical information they had accumulated, together with their license to use their patents. Their letter was sent from one department to another and was finally answered by the Board of Ordnance and Fortifications. This office, having had many proposals from inventors of flying machines, answered the letter using certain stock paragraphs refusing financial assistance. This, of course, was not at all what the Wright brothers had asked.

Although they were disappointed in the lack of interest in the machine, the Wright brothers continued with their experiments. A few short articles about their accomplishments appeared in papers and magazines from time to time. Most people were incredulous. Humans had never flown; they were never meant to fly. This was the general attitude.

Then in 1906, when the Wrights were at work on a new engine, a brief article in a New York newspaper caught the eye of Mr. E. S. Eddy, a former partner of Charles R. Flint. He thought that the Wright brothers and their invention might be of some interest to his former partner and he made a trip to Dayton to see the brothers. Mr. Eddy became acquainted with the Wrights and satisfied himself that they could be depended upon. Through his influence, the Flint firm became the Wrights' representative in all countries outside the United States. Later the Wrights themselves managed their affairs in all English-speaking countries.

By this time people in Europe, especially in France, became interested in this new machine. The brothers went to Europe to discuss their invention with prominent men. Later Wilbur made another trip to France to demonstrate the machine and teach others to operate it. Slowly but surely the whole world was becoming aware of the Wright brothers' success in fulfilling man's dream of flying.

The United States government, too, began to show interest in the invention. They offered to consider bids for a plane that could fly forty miles an hour. Bids were received from several companies, but the Wright brothers alone were able to fulfil the contract.

From then on records were made and broken in quick succession. However, the two men were as cautious as always in their experiments. As a result they had only one fatal accident. In September, 1908, while Orville was flying at the height of seventy-five feet, a propeller blade snapped in two and the machine plunged to earth. Orville suffered fractures of the thigh and ribs. His passenger, Lieutenant Thomas E. Selfridge, died three hours later from a skull fracture. That was America's first plane fatality.

Wilbur lived to see his invention gain world-wide fame, but not long enough to watch its modern development. He died on May 30, 1912, in Dayton, Ohio, when only forty-five years old. Orville Wright is still living and has continued his interest in aeronautical work.

John Paul Jones

Our First
Great Sea Fighter

JOHN PAUL JONES is one of the most exciting and colorful figures in all American history. He despised danger and did not know the meaning of the word "defeat." Commanding ships that even in his day were laughably weak and poorly equipped, he led his Yankee sailors to victory after victory with his courage and spirit.

In December, 1775, when he was commissioned a first lieutenant, the American Navy comprised only eight converted merchant ships and was therefore the butt of many an international

16

joke. By the end of the Revolutionary War our navy had gained the respect of the whole world and most of the credit must go to this one great commander, John Paul Jones.

John Paul Jones was born July 6, 1747, in Kirkcudbright, Scotland, the son of John Paul, the gardener on a large estate. Just why he later added Jones to his name no one knows.

As a child, John attended the parish school. He studied diligently, but spent every spare moment along the Solway Firth. Here he sailed small boats while envying the crew of the large sailing vessels that came and went.

At twelve, he himself became a sailor and on his first voyage traveled to Fredericksburg, Virginia. By lucky chance, he had a brother, William, living there with whom he stayed while in port.

Later John Paul served on several slavers. Running slave ships was a lawful business in those days, but he hated the task and finally decided never to take a job on another slaver.

When only twenty, he achieved the goal of all who follow the sea—he was made captain of a ship. It happened this way. John was returning to England from Jamaica, traveling as a passenger aboard a brigantine. Soon after sailing, an epidemic of yellow fever broke out and both the captain and first mate died. John Paul took command of the ship and did a notable job. As reward he was made captain by the ship's owners.

In 1773 William Paul, his brother, died. John inherited the Virginia estate and came to America to live. Soon afterward he assumed the name Jones. In spite of his humble background, the newcomer had a great deal of native intelligence. Courteous and likable, too, he quickly made many friends, including such notables as Robert Morris and Thomas Jefferson.

At the outbreak of the Revolution, Jones's first assignment was flag lieutenant on the *Alfred,* a small converted merchantman serving as Commodore Hopkins's flagship.

Aboard this ship Jones himself hoisted the first American flag to be flown from a naval vessel. It was the original flag of the Revolution—yellow background with rattlesnake and pine tree above the words, "Don't tread on me."

Jones's first independent command was the brig *Providence*, carrying seventy men and twelve four-pound guns. Though small, she was a trim ship and in four months' time Jones had destroyed enemy property worth a million dollars.

From the *Providence* he returned to the *Alfred* as commander, and with only half the normal crew made a splendid record, winning promotion to rank of Navy captain.

On June 14, 1777, Jones was ordered to the *Ranger*, a corvette carrying eighteen light guns. At the same time Congress adopted the Stars and Stripes as our national emblem. On July 4, the new United States flag was flown for the first time over any ship as Jones hoisted it on the *Ranger*. Then he sailed for European waters, carrying to France the news of Burgoyne's surrender.

It was pride in his adopted country that made him so intent on receiving a salute to the new flag from the French fleet commanded by La Motte Piquet. On February 14, 1778, he sailed into Quiberon Bay at dusk. Salutes were exchanged, but since this was the first salute to the American flag by a foreign ship and since such recognition was very important to a new country, Jones wanted to be sure that the flag had been plainly seen. Therefore, the next morning he again deliberately sailed among the French ships, receiving and returning salutes.

Two months later he captured the British sloop-of-war *Drake* in a daring battle.

The next year Jones took command of a condemned East Indiaman which he turned into a makeshift frigate, renaming her the *Bon Homme Richard* in honor of Benjamin Franklin, editor of *Poor Richard's Almanac*. Then, flying the Stars and Stripes,

The Moon Shone on the Deck of the Bon Homme Richard

he sailed for the British Isles.

A number of valuable prizes had already been taken when toward evening on September 23, 1779, the *Bon Homme Richard* encountered the *Serapis*, a fine, new, heavily armed British frigate. One of the greatest battles in naval history ensued.

As the moon rose the shooting began. Two hours later all the eighteen-pound guns on the *Richard* had been silenced, leaving only three nine-pounders to answer the fire of the powerful *Serapis*. Fires had broken out in various parts of the *Richard*. Her hull had as many holes as a sieve and water was pouring in. Only the work of a hundred English prisoners forced to man the pumps kept the craft afloat.

Still Jones refused to give up. Sailing close to the enemy he heard a voice call out, "Have you struck?"

Quick as a flash, he flung back the answer brave men will never forget, "We have not yet begun to fight!"

The three nine-pound guns were of little value but bolstered by their leader's courage, fearless men of the *Richard's* crew rained death on the enemy from the yards above, firing muskets and hurling grenades till the decks ran with blood. Suddenly there was a terrific blast. A grenade had exploded a large store of ammunition aboard the *Serapis!*

Finally the English could take no more. Though beyond repair, the *Richard* had won! Next morning she had to be abandoned and Jones took over the *Serapis*.

A reward of fifty thousand dollars was offered by the British government for the capture of Jones but no one was ever able to collect.

Following the war, John Paul Jones served for a time in the Russian navy but was careful to retain his American citizenship of which he was very proud. Receiving little credit for his efforts in Russia, he left that country after two years.

His last years were spent in Paris, where he died on July 18,

1792. A century later his body was brought back to his beloved America, and interred at Annapolis.

John Paul Jones achieved great things in the face of tremendous odds: humble birth and lowly station; inadequate equipment and indifferent support. His success was built on an unconquerable spirit, calm courage, the will to win, faith in himself and his country's cause. His name ranks high on the list of American heroes.

Kit Carson

Frontier Scout

OF ALL the scouts who helped in the building of America none played a more important part in opening up the far west than Kit Carson. He could make his way anywhere and was afraid of nothing. Even more important, he had a keen sense of responsibility. When he took on a job, he saw it through to the end. When he made a promise, he kept it. John C. Fremont once said, "With me, Carson and truth mean the same thing." Everyone felt that way about this forthright and capable man.

Christopher Houston Carson was born on December 24, 1809, in Madison County, Kentucky, but he grew up in Howard County, Missouri, where his family moved when he was a year old.

Life in Missouri was rude and rough and the trappers who came to visit the Carsons were rough and uncouth, too. On their return from trapping trips more than one of them showed off an Indian scalp or two along with their beaver furs.

Learning to ride, shoot and use a knife was considered much more important than reading and writing in this wild country, and Kit became expert at all three before he was twelve. Someone taught him to write his name, but he never went to school.

At fifteen the boy became a saddler's apprentice, but in less than a year he ran away to join a wagon train headed for Santa Fe. Reaching Santa Fe safely, Kit went on to Taos where many trappers lived. There a friendly old fellow named Kincaid gave him a home. That winter Kit learned to speak Spanish and also picked up a lot of information about trapping in the Rockies.

Twice during the next year Kit started home for Missouri but each time turned back. Finally in 1829 he got the chance he had been waiting for—he was asked to join a party of trappers. Just imagine his excitement when he heard they were going to California!

The leader of the party, Ewing Young, was an old Indian fighter. One day a scout reported that Indians in war paint were headed their way. Young told most of the trappers to hide in the underbrush. Seeing only the few that were left, the whooping Indians rushed forward. The remaining trappers dove into the underbrush, the Indians close behind. Then suddenly there was a roar of guns. Fifteen redskins fell. Realizing that they had been tricked, the rest of the Indians turned and fled.

A week or two later the trappers reached the Mission of San Gabriel, not far from El Pueblo de Nuestra Senora La Reina de Los Angeles. This was then a tiny Mexican settlement; now the great city of Los Angeles is built on the same site.

Never had Kit seen such beauty and abundance. To celebrate their arrival in California the trappers had a big barbecue. They exchanged four knives for a whole steer and were given besides all kinds of fruits and vegetables.

During their trek north from San Gabriel, Kit led two successful battles with the Indians, and by the time he returned to Santa Fe, he had more than proved his cleverness and daring.

From then on, Carson was asked many times to trap for established companies, but he liked to work with a small party of his own.

Every summer all the trappers gathered at some rendezvous where traders also came with provisions and supplies. There was always plenty of whiskey on sale and none indulged more freely than a French-Canadian bully named Shuman.

One day Shuman became more insulting than usual, and shouted that all Americans were spineless and yellow, that he could lick any one of them with one arm tied behind him.

Kit soon grew tired of all this bragging. Stepping up to Shuman he said quietly, "If you're looking for a fight, I'll be glad to accommodate you."

A few minutes later the two men rode toward each other from opposite ends of the camp. Shuman fired first, grazing Kit's head. Then Kit fired, smashing the bone in Shuman's right elbow so that the bully could never fight again.

At the end of the 1834 trapping season, Carson was surprised to discover that his furs were worth only half as much as they had been other years. For a long time beaver pelts had brought a good price because the fur was used for making men's hats. Now Carson was told that styles had changed. Eastern men were wearing silk instead of beaver hats.

Carson then became hunter for Fort Bent in Colorado. He kept this job for eight years, killing thousands of buffalo and other game. One day while he was hunting, he had a narrow escape. He had just shot a large elk and was heading toward the animal when he saw a big grizzly bear heading toward *him*. There was no time to reload his gun so he ran for a near-by tree. Swinging into the branches he hastily broke off a limb. As the bear started up the tree after him, Kit reached down and rapped the animal smartly on the nose. The grizzly dropped to the ground, but seconds later was back. Kit hit him again. Again the bear retreated. This performance was repeated at least a dozen times before the grizzly suddenly got wind of the dead elk. Here was something he could get at without opposition. So he ate his fill and finally lumbered away into the woods.

While at Fort Bent, Carson married a beautiful Comanche Indian girl. She died a year later but left Kit a lovely little daughter. When the child reached school age, her father took her to St. Louis to place her in a good school.

On his way back to Colorado, Carson met Lieutenant John C. Fremont, just setting out on an exploration trip to the Rockies. The two men became friends and Fremont asked Carson to join the party.

Carson was with Fremont much of the time during the next five years. He accompanied him on three expeditions. The first was comparatively unimportant, but the second took them north to Oregon and then south to Sutter's Fort on the Sacramento. On the third trip they went to the coast where they took part in the war against Mexico.

Fremont's reports were full of praise for Carson's honesty and ability. He credited the scout with much of the success of his expeditions.

In 1847, Carson was sent to Washington with dispatches. The social life of the capital amazed Carson. He had a good time but was glad to get back to the simple frontier life.

Carson had married again and spent the last twenty years of his life in or near Taos, ranching and trapping. He served for a time as Indian agent and was commanding officer of a New Mexico regiment during the Civil War.

In the spring of 1868, he went north to visit a son in Colorado. There on May 23 he died.

Thomas A. Edison

Miracle Man of Electricity

WHEN YOU have read the story of Thomas Edison and all his wonderful inventions, you'll probably say, "He must have been a magician!" or "There never was a greater genius!"

People used to say things like that to Edison himself and to one of them he drily replied, "Genius is two percent *inspiration* and ninety-eight percent *perspiration*."

Certainly, few people have ever worked as hard as this great man. He seldom slept more than four or five hours a night and one time worked five days and five nights without leaving his laboratory!

And what were the results of all this labor? It would take hours just to name them all, but here are a few examples: the incandescent lamp or electric light bulb we all use in our homes; the phonograph; the first practical motion picture camera; the

26

quadruplex telegraph which makes it possible to send two messages in each direction over the same wire at the same time; a new kind of transmitter for the Bell telephone which made it practical for everyday use. In all, Edison secured 1,033 patents during his lifetime and Congress placed a value of over fifteen billion dollars on his inventions.

Thomas Alva Edison was born in Milan, Ohio, on February 11, 1847, the seventh and youngest son of Samuel Edison. He was of Dutch and Scotch ancestry.

From the time he could talk, the child wanted to know the "how" and "why" of everything, and when only six, the story goes, he tried his first "experiment." After getting full details from his mother as to how baby goslings were hatched, he disappeared from the house. Going in search of him later his mother was both amazed and amused to find him in the barn, patiently sitting on a nest of goose eggs. It took some time to persuade him that he could not possibly take the mother goose's place.

The following year the Edison family moved to Port Huron, Michigan, and young Tom was sent to school. His mother, an ex-teacher who had taught him to read, knew he had a fine mind, but at school Tom always seemed to be at the foot of the class. After three months he went to school no more but was tutored by his mother. Before he reached his teens he was reading such books as Hume's "History of England" and Gibbon's "Decline and Fall of the Roman Empire."

At twelve, Tom got a job as train boy on the Grand Trunk Railroad, selling candy, peanuts and newspapers. Soon he started publishing a small weekly paper of his own, setting up his little hand press in the baggage car. Tom's paper was so interesting and unusual he soon had a subscription list of over four hundred.

Besides the press he kept various chemicals in the baggage car for odd-moment experiments. One day a jar of phosphorous fell and broke, causing a small fire. The angry conductor put Tom and all his belongings off the train at the next stop, boxing the boy's ears as he left. The blow made Edison permanently deaf in one ear.

The boy's laboratory was then transferred to his home where he carefully labeled all bottles and jars "poison" to frighten off any possible meddlers.

At fifteen, Edison was taught telegraphy as a reward for rescuing the son of a telegraph operator from the path of a swift moving train. He then went to work as a night telegraph operator and during the next five years held similar jobs in nine different cities.

Edison's first patent, taken out in 1868, covered an electrical vote recorder. He found no market for it and from then on spent his efforts only on things for which there was a demand. He had no time for waste motion.

When about twenty-two he invented an improved stock ticker and planned to ask five thousand dollars for the patent. However, fearing this might be considered too much, he asked the interested financier to make him an offer.

"Forty thousand dollars," came the prompt reply. This sum enabled Edison to set up a real laboratory, and he began to produce as never before.

While experimenting on his carbon transmitter for the telephone, Edison discovered the principle of the talking machine. Even his own staff laughed at this idea, but Edison persisted. The first model was a tinfoil-covered cylinder which turned with a hand crank. Crude, yes, but what excitement it caused! It seemed that everyone in America, from the President down, wanted to see and hear this marvelous machine. Later Edison developed a motor-driven machine with cylindrical wax records.

In the 1870's electric arc lights were known but were too bright and big for use in the home. Edison undertook the task of developing a new type of electric light known as the incandescent lamp. In his search for a filament he carbonized and tried to use paper and cotton and literally thousands of different materials. At last after many months he succeeded with a strip of bamboo from a Japanese fan. For ten years after this the filaments in all incandescent lamps were made from carbonized bamboo.

Edison knew nothing about photography when he started working on his kinetoscope or motion picture camera, but he quickly learned all he needed to know and went on from there. The inventor also did some work on talking motion pictures in 1894, although commercially successful sound pictures came much later.

In recognition of his contributions to humanity, Edison was given honorary awards by many countries.

America's greatest inventor died in his eighty-fifth year, on October 18, 1931, at his home in West Orange, New Jersey.

George Washington

Father of His Country

EACH YEAR on February 22nd we observe the anniversary of the birth of the one man who could successfully have led our country in its struggle for independence. This man — George Washington — so strong-willed and determined, so filled with faith and strength of character, richly deserves his foremost place in America's Hall of Fame.

George Washington was born in 1752, the fifth child of Augustine Washington, a well-to-do Virginia planter. We do not know much about his early boyhood, which probably explains why so many fables have developed about him.

Those fables picture him as somewhat of a prig or a sissy. In truth, he was neither. He was a normal, healthy boy who loved the outdoors and whose great strength enabled him to excel in such sports as wrestling and weight-lifting. The people whom he knew were not afraid to be gay and to enjoy life. Although

there was an established religion—the Church of England—and
the law required everyone to attend Sunday worship regularly,
most of the clergy believed in wholesome recreation and often
joined in the fun.

George had little schooling, and throughout his life his spelling and grammar remained poor. Like many another boy, he
kept a notebook and in this, at one time, he wrote down one
hundred and ten rules for polite conduct. Some, like the warning not to eat meat with one's knife, nor to pick one's teeth with
a fork, probably indicate that the table manners of the day were
commonly not very good.

Apparently determined that his penmanship should be of the
best, he practiced until he had developed a fine hand. As a
youth, he wrote some poetry, much of it inspired by young
ladies in whom he was interested.

His big, well-proportioned body he made to serve him well
in dancing and sports. Besides wrestling and weight-lifting, he
liked to pitch quoits, and is said to have been able to throw a
dollar, or a stone (probably a stone), across the Rappahannock.
He early became an excellent horseman, often breaking in thor-
oughbred colts for their owners. The story is told that he once
rode a colt to its death when the animal refused to give in to
him. Certainly he was a graceful rider, capable of tirelessly
spending hour after hour in the saddle, whether traveling, hunting or leading his troops.

While in his teens, George had been taken by his brother,
Lawrence, to live with him on Lawrence's large estate. There
he became acquainted, and was very popular, with the Fair-
faxes and others of Virginia's wealthy families. He became interested in surveying and, as an assistant surveyor, accompanied
a group into the forest to lay out boundaries in the wilderness.

Young Washington's diary tells of his interesting experiences
on that trip. He slept on the ground, under only one blanket,

which, according to him, bore double its weight in lice and fleas. Sometimes, the men were able to sleep under haystacks. When someone shot a wild turkey, they feasted, serving the food on large chips of wood. Once a party of Indians was en-couraged by the fun-loving surveyors to perform a war dance, which amused Washington a great deal.

A little later, Washington secured a post as public surveyor for the county, at an annual salary of $100—quite a sum of money in those days. This he held for some time, spending his leisure in hunting, dancing and good living.

When Washington was only twenty-one, Governor Dinwiddie appointed him Adjutant General, with the rank of major, in charge of one of Virginia's four military districts. He learned to fence, and spent much time studying the art of war.

By this time, Washington had attained his full physical growth. He has been described as a giant of a man, over six feet tall, with a handsome, well-shaped head. His widely set, blue-gray eyes could be stern and commanding on occasion. His mouth was ordinarily held firmly closed, even then, and that firmness was later accentuated, as is shown in portraits, because of the difficulty he had in keeping his false teeth properly fixed in his mouth. Artificial teeth were very rough and usually un-comfortable in Washington's time.

Washington first attained some fame outside of Virginia as a result of taking part in the French and Indian Wars as a colonel of militia. Before the war actually started, he had been sent with a small force to warn the French out of western Pennsylvania, which was claimed as British territory. Meeting greatly superior French forces, he was unsuccessful, but acquitted himself well. Later on, he was made General Braddock's aide and accompan-ied Braddock on the expedition which ended so disastrously for the British cause. When Braddock was killed, Washington, through his coolness and skill, helped to save the remnants of the British and American troops. It was in this engagement that Washington himself escaped death in so seemingly miraculous a fashion, two horses being shot from under him and his uniform pierced by enemy bullets.

Returning from the war, Washington married Martha Custis, a widow, who was widely respected for her charming manner. Then he settled down at his Mount Vernon estate to devote himself to the life of a gentleman farmer. He was hard-working and successful, becoming one of the wealthiest men in the colonies.

Eminent as he was, he naturally went into public life. He was elected to the Virginia House of Burgesses and became a leading figure in the politics of the colony. By 1769, a show-down with King George III's government in England over the question of taxation was looming. Washington urged resistance by the colonists, although at that time, like most other leading Americans, he had no thought of a complete break and independence.

He was chosen, with Patrick Henry and Edmund Pendleton, to represent Virginia at the First Continental Congress. Then, when the Second Continental Congress met, Washington appeared wearing the uniform of a Virginia colonel. He was ready to meet the crisis, and the Congress responded by making him the commander of the Continental Army.

Washington, having announced that he would serve without pay, immediately proceeded to Boston to take over the command of the patriot forces in that area. The Battle of Bunker Hill had already been fought, and the patriots were keeping the British penned up in the city of Boston.

The new commander was dismayed at his army. They lacked uniforms. Many were deserting, partly, it is true, to go home and tend to their farm work. There was an excess of officers, but, on the other hand, discipline was poor.

Nevertheless, Washington, with characteristic determination, did his best and managed to whip the untrained men into the semblance of an organized fighting force. Then, in a sudden move which caught the British by surprise, he placed his cannon on the high land overlooking Boston. The British were forced to evacuate the city and, embarking in their vessels, sailed for New York.

Anticipating the British move, Washington hurried his army to New York also, arriving there first. Congress ordered him to hold the city—an impossible task, since it was surrounded by water and Washington had no fleet. Against his better judgment, he attempted to carry out his orders. In the Battle of Long Island, his green troops were outflanked and cut to pieces by the British regulars and the Hessian soldiers hired by the British King. Due to the slowness of General Howe, Washington very fortunately was able to get part of his army back on the mainland. Otherwise, the Revolution might have ended then and there.

The long retreat across New Jersey began. This was indeed a testing time for Washington. He had suffered a bad defeat. Many people gave up hope. The patriot cause seemed lost. Washington knew that some of his officers were complaining about him and that groups in Congress were working to replace him. Unfaltering, he retained his steadfast calmness. His own very real worries he suppressed. He prayed, and drawing on his great store of common sense and faith, he gave faith and confidence to others.

The campaign had gone into the winter, so conditions were unfavorable for fighting. However, Washington knew that the patriot cause needed a victory to restore lagging spirits. The surprise attack, now famous as the crossing of the Deleware, on the Hessians quartered at Trenton on Christmas Day, 1776, provided the victory. A few days later, Washington, by a daring ruse, eluded General Cornwallis's regulars and took Princeton. The New Jersey campaign established Washington as a brilliant field commander and gave the Americans new hope and courage.

For the duration of the war, Washington had little chance to exhibit daring in the field. He could not prevent the British from taking Philadelphia, nor could he recapture New York. But he held the patriot army together through the bitter winters at Morristown and Valley Forge. He kept troops in the field, in spite of disheartening desertions, poor supplies and political opposition. He spent his own money when Congress was slow in supplying funds. He gave unsparingly of himself, and he inspired in his followers love and great respect.

After the British surrender at Yorktown, Washington knew the fighting was over and yearned to retire. A group of his officers proposed to overthrow Congress and make him king, but he rejected the idea with scorn. In December, 1782, he resigned his commission and returned to Mount Vernon, hoping to spend the rest of his days in peace and quiet. There, he was besieged by friends and by artists—painters and sculptors who had come to make likenesses of the great man. He learned to endure the long sittings with patience.

At the end of the war, and often thereafter, Washington said that the country needed a stronger central government. It was not surprising that he was chosen to preside over the Philadelphia Convention of 1787, called to make a new Constitution. And no one wanted any other than Washington as the first President.

His journey from Mount Vernon to New York for the inauguration was a triumphal one. Crowds surged along the gaily decorated route, and flowers were strewn in his path. Troops and special committees turned out to greet him.

In New York, he was welcomed by waving flags, ringing bells and roaring cannon. He took the oath of office on a balcony in full sight of thousands. Then Robert Livingston shouted, "Long live George Washington, President of the United States." People cheered madly, the Stars and Stripes were raised and the cannon on the ships in the harbor boomed salvo after salvo.

Washington, skilled in military matters, knew little of the problems of civil government. Realizing this, he applied himself diligently to the study of official papers and was wise enough to surround himself with able men as the heads of the departments in the new government.

The first President successfully guided the affairs of the nation for four years and then, although he longed to return to farming at Mount Vernon, he yielded to the popular demand that he serve another term. However, he felt the attacks of critics keenly and resisted all entreaties that he accept a third term. So, in 1797, he at last returned to his estate and spent his few remaining years quietly—happy to watch a grateful nation growing in strength and vigor, and secure in the knowledge that he had done so much to give it strength.

On a December day in 1799, they laid to rest the mortal remains of George Washington. The plaudits and cheers of the crowd were no longer his; but in their place came then the quiet tribute and the reverence which Americans will always render to his memory.

John James Audubon

America's Favorite Naturalist

SINCE THE beginning of time, birds have been a source of interest to man. Their freedom, their songs and colors, and the beauty of their flight have always fascinated earth-bound mortals. But in spite of this interest no one had ever made a real study of birds and their habits before John James Audubon began his work.

Through his own efforts Audubon became an ornithologist, which is just another way of saying he became an expert on birds. He was the first person to visit their haunts and to learn their secrets. This he did through long and patient observation, often lying for hours with a telescope watching one small bird build a nest or feed its young.

Audubon was gifted with a talent for painting, too, and his

great work, *The Birds of America*, includes 1,065 pictures of birds, beautiful and accurate in every detail. This collection still holds its place as one of the finest of its kind.

Historians disagree about the exact place and date of Audubon's birth. Some say he was born in Louisiana on May 4 or 5, 1780; others say he was born in Santo Domingo on April 26, 1785. Whichever is correct, he was the son of Jean Audubon, a French sea captain and adventurer.

While still very young, the child was taken to France by his father. There his early education was arranged by an indulgent stepmother who did not emphasize the importance of formal schooling. He learned some mathematics, geography, music and fencing but the only lessons he enjoyed were those given him in drawing by the French artist, Jacques Louis David.

A trip to the country was the boy's greatest joy. He would wander happily through the woods for hours, gathering birds' nests and eggs, bits of wood and rock and other specimens of nature. He also expressed a desire to collect birds.

His father, who had planned a military career for his son, did his best to discourage this absorbing interest in nature, but finally gave up. At the age of fifteen, John had collected about two hundred French birds and was making drawings of them.

Trained in no particular trade or profession, the youth was sent to America in 1803 to manage an estate near Philadelphia owned by his father. The estate got little attention, but in the woods and valleys near by young Audubon found new worlds to conquer. Soon all the shelves and tables in the house were covered with stuffed specimens of new and fascinating birds, and he began the careful study which ultimately resulted in the publication of *The Birds of America*.

Returning to France, he served for a short time in the French navy, then returned to America.. Here in 1808 he married Lucy Bakewell, a highly intelligent and plucky young woman.

Shortly after their marriage, the Audubons moved to Kentucky. In their new home Audubon tried to make a living as a trader, but having no aptitude for business, turned to painting portraits and teaching fencing. Every spare moment he spent wandering through forests, seeking new birds to paint.

After a time he journeyed to Louisiana to study the birdlife there. Many times he went hungry, but he was always ready to help another person if he possibly could. One day a poor barefooted man asked him for help in getting shoes. Audubon had no money and his own shoes were worn completely through, but by painting the portraits of a cobbler and his wife he earned shoes for them both.

During this period his family remained in Kentucky, but about 1821 they came to Louisiana, too. Mrs. Audubon had great faith in her husband and persuaded him to leave the family's support to her while he devoted all his time to studying and painting birds. She soon had a teaching position.

Five years later Audubon went to England to exhibit his drawings and paintings. By securing pledges of one thousand dollars each from a hundred Englishmen, he finally had his paintings published along with descriptive articles about each bird. First editions of the various volumes of *The Birds of America* appeared between 1827 and 1838.

Following his return to America, Audubon bought an estate on the Hudson River. He spent part of his time there and part in long trips gathering material about birds and animals.

About 1846 Audubon's health began to fail and he gradually became weaker. He died at his home in New York on January 27, 1851, and is buried in Trinity Cemetery.

Today there are Audubon Societies all over North America with a membership of seventy-five thousand in the United States alone. The purpose of these societies is to educate people to appreciate and protect bird life.

Sam Houston

Lone Star Soldier and Statesman

No SINGLE person in American history exerted greater influence over a state's destiny than did Sam Houston over that of Texas. He not only led the Texans to victory against great odds in their fight for independence from Mexico, but also guided Texas through the nine trying years that preceded its admission to the Union.

Truly representative of the vast territory he loved so well, this famous Texan had all the color, dash and verve of a Western adventurer combined with the smooth charm of a Southern gentleman.

Samuel Houston, known as "Sam," was born March 2, 1793, in Rockbridge County, Virginia. Sam Houston, his father, had been an officer in the Continental Army and was later an in-

40

spector of army outposts. He died when young Sam was thirteen years old, leaving Mrs. Houston with nine dependent children.

Less courageous women might have given way before the problems which faced her, but Sam's mother had all the spirit and determination of a true pioneer. Gathering together her household goods, she moved her family across the Alleghenies to Tennessee. With the help of her sons she built a log cabin not far from the favorite hunting grounds of the Cherokee Indians.

Schools were few and far between in the new territory. Sam liked to read, particularly adventure stories, and he read every book he could get.

The boy worked for a time in a frontier store, but finally gave up his job to explore the land of the Cherokees. Here he struck up a friendship with several Indian youths and soon was accepted among all the tribe. Hunting and fishing with his new friends, learning their language, living in their homes for long periods, he developed a sympathetic understanding of the race. In later years as a United States Senator, he did his utmost to establish friendly relations between the white men and red men.

The colorful clothes of the Indians appealed to young Houston, and he took to wearing brightly flowered hunting shirts. He also let his hair grow long and wore it in a queue down his back.

At eighteen, he established a country school near his mother's home, charging his pupils eight dollars a year tuition. The larger part of the tuition was paid in goods, but many children attended the school and the young man did very well.

During the War of 1812 Houston fought under General Andrew Jackson and took part in his campaign against the Creeks. In attempting to drive a band of Indians from a heavily wooded ravine, Houston received a severe wound which troubled him all his life.

After a year as sub-agent of the Cherokees, the young pioneer studied law and was admitted to the bar, soon becoming one of the region's leading lawyers.

In 1819 he was elected district attorney for the Nashville district. Shortly afterward he was made major general of the militia, then elected and re-elected to Congress, and twice chosen governor of Tennessee.

Houston had married, but when his marriage turned out unhappily, he resigned as governor and went to live with the Cherokees in their newly established reservation. Kindly received, he stayed with them for some years, acting as their adviser and spokesman.

In 1832, President Andrew Jackson needed someone to negotiate with the Texas Indians in an attempt to stop raids on the border settlements and called on Houston as the man best qualified for this work. Houston readily accepted.

Texas, which now comprises one-twelfth the entire area of the United States, was at that time part of Mexico. Early exploration of the territory had been made by Spanish adventurers from Mexico in the 1500's. After Mexico gained her independence from Spain many Americans migrated to Texas, attracted by offers of free land. The newcomers sought to strengthen Texas's position in the Mexican republic. Turning down their petitions, President Santa Anna also attempted to disarm them. The settlers voted for rebellion, and in 1834 Houston became leader of the Texan army.

Early in 1836 one hundred and fifty Texans were attacked by four thousand Mexicans in the historic battle of the Alamo. All but seven of the defenders were killed and when the seven finally surrendered, they were cruelly massacred.

"Remember the Alamo!" became the rallying cry of the angry

One Hundred and Fifty Texans Defended the Alamo

Texans. A few months later independence was theirs as seven hundred forty-three of their untrained troops completely routed sixteen hundred Mexican veterans in the battle of San Jacinto.

Houston was elected president of the new Texas republic and proved an able executive. He established law and order, secured early recognition of his government by the United States, made friends of the Indians and finally, after three attempts, gained Texas's admission to the Union in 1845.

Following twelve years in the United States Senate, Houston became governor of Texas in 1859. However, two years later he was removed from office because he refused to join the Confederacy against the Union.

Sam Houston was sure his state's secession was a grave mistake. Distressed and disheartened, he retired to his home at Huntsville, where he died on July 26, 1863.

The city of Houston, Texas, was named in honor of this colorful figure of frontier days.

Robert E. Peary

Discoverer of the North Pole

ROBERT E. PEARY's discovery of the North Pole will surely remain as one of the most thrilling achievements of this century. More than five hundred expeditions from many different countries had gone before him and failed. Scores of men had lost their lives in the search. Peary himself had had to turn back five times, but dogged determination and long years of effort finally tipped the scales in his favor. On April 6, 1909, he reached his goal and planted the American flag on the northernmost part of the world.

Robert Edwin Peary was born at Cresson Springs, Pennsylvania, on May 6, 1856. When his father died three years later, Mrs. Peary took little Robert and returned to her girlhood home in Portland, Maine.

From the time he was just a tiny lad Robert loved the out-of-doors. As he grew older, he and his friends spent every out-of-school hour on Portland's bustling waterfront. What fun it was to wander along the wharves, watching the dock hands unload the ships, listening to sailors' tales of far-off lands, talking with fishermen as they mended their nets! And when they wanted some active sport—what could be better than swimming and fishing?

Following graduation from Bowdoin College, young Peary spent four years as a surveyor in the little town of Fryeburg, Maine. Surrounded by gorgeous mountain country, Peary spent many happy hours hiking and fishing for mountain trout.

Life in Fryeburg was extremely pleasant, but after four years Peary had worked himself out of a job. Since there was no more demand for a surveyor, Peary decided to try for a job as civil engineer in the Navy. He passed his examination with flying colors and was made a lieutenant.

Several years later, while out for an evening stroll in Washington, Peary wandered into an old book shop where he loved to browse. When still a boy, Peary had read a book by Elisha Kane telling about Kane's voyages in the Arctic Ocean. The book had thrilled him and he had talked about it for weeks. Now, in thumbing through the piles of dusty books and periodicals in the book shop, Peary found an article about Greenland and the great ice sheet which covers most of this northern island. As he read it, all that Kane had written came back. He read other books on Greenland and the Arctic. He soon had a great longing to visit the north and see life there for himself. Realizing that reading alone would never satisfy him, he arranged for a leave so that he could make a trip there.

Peary's first trip to Greenland was made in the summer of 1886. Most of the people who live on the island are Eskimos. Even in the southernmost part it is very cold nearly the whole

year round. The interior is mountainous and covered with gla-
ciers. Few of us would choose a country like this for a vacation,
but Peary was enthralled and left determined to return again.

The opportunity came three years later, shortly after Peary's
marriage. Mrs. Peary went along on this trip and on the next
one, when their daughter was born. Everyone called the little
girl "the Snow Baby" because she was the first white child born
so far north in this ice-covered country.

Between trips, Peary told many thrilling stories of walrus
hunting in the Arctic. The walrus weighs two thousand pounds
or more and is always ready to pick a fight. Sometimes,
Peary said, a whole herd would attack a single whaleboat, trying to climb aboard or to punch holes in the boat with their
sharp tusks. Such excitement there would be as half the men
swung boat hooks and clubs to keep the walruses out of the boat
while the other half fired away with their guns.

On his first three trips, Peary's main interest was Greenland.
Then in 1898 he made his first attempt to reach the North Pole
but was forced back. Four more times he tried and failed. Mis-
fortune hounded him, but he refused to give up. On each trip
he added to his knowledge of the frigid land. He was certain
that if only he persisted he must succeed.

In July of 1908 Peary sailed from America in a ship especially
built for the Arctic regions. It was called the *Roosevelt*. Though
the water was full of icebergs, the ship was able to sail all the
way to Cape Sheridan, about five hundred miles from the
North Pole.

Leaving the *Roosevelt*, the explorer set out on February 15,
1909, with sixty-six men, one hundred forty Eskimo dogs and
twenty-three sledges. All of the men were dressed in fur from
head to toe.

The ice fields before them were jagged and rough. Every
foot forward was a struggle. Though all of the men were strong

and husky, several had had to give up by the end of the week. As the battle against the elements continued, others also were sent back to the base. By the time Peary had reached a latitude of eighty-eight degrees, 138 miles from the Pole, he had cut down his party to five men, five sledges and about thirty dogs.

Now for the final dash. Success was in sight and the four Eskimos and one Negro who remained with Peary were as pleased and excited as he.

But there were still dangers to overcome. One day, for example, Peary came to a place where the ice was starting to split apart to form a channel. Many places there was a yard or more of open water between cakes of ice. If they did not hurry they might have to go miles around. Peary went ahead, testing each cake of ice to make sure it would hold the dogs and sledges without tilting. Then he would turn to urge the dogs on while the driver steered the sledge behind. For awhile it seemed impossible that all could make it, but luckily they did.

That was one of the last hazards. Early on April 6, 1909, the little party, thin and worn, reached the Pole. Peary had realized his dream at last—he was standing on top of the world.

The party stayed at the Pole until the next afternoon, taking pictures and making scientific observations. During this time the temperature ranged from twelve below zero to thirty-three below zero.

Not long after his return to the United States the explorer was given the rank of rear admiral in the United States Navy. He was honored throughout the world for his triumph.

Admiral Robert E. Peary died February 19, 1920, at the age of sixty-three.

Good-Will Ambassador

WILL ROGERS was America's "Prince of Wit and Wisdom." He made people laugh, and he made them think, too. He had an uncanny understanding of men and happenings and could say more in a few words than many statesmen could in an hour-long speech. He had little use for stuffed shirts or snobs and liked nothing better than "to take the wind out of the sails" of the country's bigwigs. Yet the fun he poked was never malicious. People were usually proud to say they had been joshed by Will Rogers.

Few Americans have been more beloved. It was a cold person, indeed, who did not respond to the warmth of this friendly, unassuming man. He had friends all over the world, and his principle charm lay in the fact that he never failed to practice what he preached: "Be yourself!"

Always the gentleman, Rogers never pretended to be a scholar. Although well educated, he preferred to put his remarks in an ungrammatical style that encouraged his listeners and readers to laugh at and with him. "All I know is what I read in the papers," he'd drawl, usually following the statement with a sage observation on some world event.

Will Rogers (christened William Penn Adair Rogers) was born near what is now Claremore, Oklahoma, on November 4, 1879, the eighth and youngest child of Clement Vann Rogers, prosperous rancher and banker. Both Will's parents were part Cherokee Indian and he was always very proud of this ancestry. As he later told a Boston audience, "My ancestors didn't come over on the Mayflower—they met the boat."

As a boy, life on the range suited Will to a T. He became a wonderful rider and an expert with a lasso, roping everything in sight, including his sisters. Most of his time was spent out-of-doors and it was no easy job to try to settle down when his father sent him away to school—first to the Willie Halsell College in Vinita, Oklahoma, and later to Kemper Military Academy in Missouri.

Discipline at the academy was especially strict and Will heartily disliked wearing a uniform. Finally he decided he had all he could stand and wrote each of his sisters of his desperate need for ten dollars. When the money arrived, Will made off for Texas. After a short time in the oil fields, however, he was glad to return home.

Soon afterward Will organized a small rodeo, taking part in the roping and other contests. The show lost money, but Will found the field in which he belonged—the show business.

During the next few years he performed in rodeos, a circus, wild west shows and in 1905 broke into "big time" at Hammerstein's Roof Garden in New York. His act was booked as a rope twirling act, and he was among the best with a lasso, but it was his droll remarks which set people saying, "You ought to hear that Western fellow. He's *good!*"

In a few years' time, Will Rogers had become the theater's foremost humorist. Invariably chewing gum as he spun his lariat, he carried on a monologue of homespun philosophy that enchanted listeners from every walk of life. Presidents and princes laughed right along with butchers and bakers when Will Rogers performed.

He became top star of the Ziegfield Follies and with the advent of radio and talking pictures his drawling voice and frank open face became familiar to Americans everywhere. He was a smash success, yet it was typical that just as he was becoming established in talking pictures he should set aside his own career in order to help his good friend, Fred Stone.

Stone had broken both legs in an airplane crash just after the opening of one of his plays. The show was about to close when Rogers wired that he would be glad to "pinch hit" until Stone was well. A scheduled picture had to be postponed for months but with Rogers, friends came first. His own work could wait.

For several years, the first thing millions of Americans read in their daily newspapers was a witty paragraph headed "Will Rogers Says—." The humorist also wrote many magazine articles and a number of books. He was a favorite on the lecture platform, and no after-dinner speaker ever drew more applause.

Though constantly in the limelight himself, Will Rogers insisted on privacy for his family. His wife was the former Betty Blake whom he married in 1908. They became the parents of three children, Will Jr., Mary and James.

An inveterate traveler, Rogers was modern aviation's greatest booster and is reputed to have flown approximately 500,000 miles as a passenger.

He had many friends among fliers, including Wiley Post, a fellow Oklahoman. In early August, 1935, Rogers and

Post took off on a vacation trip to the Orient, traveling in Post's red monoplane. All went well until August 15. Then as they neared Point Barrow, Alaska, engine trouble developed and, with an Eskimo hunter as lone spectator, the plane crashed in a shallow river. Both Rogers and Post were instantly killed. News of the tragedy caused mourning throughout the nation, and the memory of wise and witty Will Rogers is still held dear by millions of Americans.

Father of
American Democracy

THOMAS JEFFERSON wrote the Declaration of Independence.

If there were nothing else to say about Thomas Jefferson—if his whole story could be told in that single line—his name and fame would still endure through all American history. But in addition to writing this immortal document, the cornerstone of our democracy, Thomas Jefferson achieved much more.

With the purchase of the great Louisiana Territory while he was president, he more than doubled the size of the United States. He brought freedom of worship to Virginia. He encouraged the idea of many small farms as opposed to a few vast estates. He urged education for all and worked for better school systems. He was "Father of the University of Virginia."

Thomas Jefferson was born April 13, 1743, at Shadwell, Albemarle County, Virginia. His parents were people of wealth and refinement. His father, Peter J. Jefferson, was a planter. His mother was a member of the aristocratic Randolph family, leaders in the state's social circles.

As a child, Thomas seldom left the big plantation where he lived with his parents and seven younger brothers and sisters. Tutors were engaged to teach the boy and he received a thorough schooling in Latin, Greek, French and mathematics.

When seventeen years old, Thomas entered William and Mary College in Williamsburg, then the capital of Virginia. Here he studied law and applied himself so diligently that he sometimes spent fifteen hours a day on his studies.

While attending college, young Jefferson became acquainted with Patrick Henry and heard a number of his brilliant speeches. From then on he was as anti-British as anyone in the colony.

Not until he had studied law for five years did Jefferson apply for his license to practice. This was quite unusual, for at that time many a man opened a law office after only a few months of study.

Although the young lawyer was not a good speaker, he was very successful in his profession. This was fortunate since, when Jefferson was fourteen, his father had died, leaving him head of the family.

As he prospered, Jefferson enlarged his inherited estate and on top of its highest hill built a lovely home. He himself designed the place and called it Monticello, which means little mountain. Soon afterward, he married a wealthy young widow, Martha Wayles Skelton. Together they owned over forty thousand acres of land and more than five hundred slaves.

During his life, Jefferson worked hard for emancipation of the slaves, but he could not overcome the opposition of other big slave-holders. He himself was very kind to his slaves and set up for them a sort of trade school, teaching them to be bricklayers, smiths, cabinetmakers and masons.

Although Jefferson loved nothing more than he did his home, much unhappiness came to him there. Four of his six children died while very young, and Mrs. Jefferson passed away, too, only twelve years after their marriage.

At the time he started practicing law, Jefferson was a long-geared, large-boned, slim and erect young man of twenty-four years. He was six feet, two inches tall, with angular features, sandy hair, a ruddy complexion and hazel-flecked gray eyes.

He played the violin well, enjoyed dancing and was a gay figure at social gatherings. He was fond of fishing and hunting and was an excellent swimmer and horseman.

Few people know that Jefferson was interested in science, or that he devised many practical and amusing gadgets. For example, he built a bed into the wall between his dining room and his library, so that he could easily either start the day with breakfast or do some reading and writing first, according to the way he felt. He invented a new kind of plow, and a nail-making machine.

His election to the Virginia House of Burgesses in 1769 marked the beginning of Jefferson's career as a statesman. His ability as a writer soon became evident, and he was asked to draw up a number of important resolutions.

In 1775, Washington left the Continental Congress to take command of the Continental army, and Jefferson replaced him as delegate from Virginia. The following spring a committee was named to draw up the Declaration of Independence. Jefferson was only thirty-two years old, one of the youngest members of the Congress, but he was made chairman and was asked to do the actual writing of the document.

No better man could have been chosen, not only because of his gift for terse and forceful writing, but also because of his earnest and deep belief in the people and in their right to life, liberty and the pursuit of happiness.

What a proud and happy moment it must have been for this ardent patriot when the Declaration, practically as he had written it, was accepted and signed by Congress!

There was no telegraph then to flash the great news throughout the world, but as soon as copies could be printed, the Declaration of Independence was carried by special couriers on horseback to all the thirteen colonies.

Jefferson could have continued as a member of the Congress, but he preferred to return to the Virginia legislature to work for certain reforms he believed urgent.

For example, up until this time, all Virginians were required to attend the Church of England. Jefferson believed the people should have the right to choose their own churches and was instrumental in securing that freedom for them.

One after another, Jefferson brought about important changes in Virginia's laws to conform with his democratic principles. He made many enemies in the process, but he knew he was right and never backed down.

Jefferson later served as governor of Virginia for two years and in 1783 returned to Congress. The following year he was sent to France to help negotiate commercial treaties and remained to serve as minister to that country after Benjamin Franklin's retirement.

On this occasion the French prime minister greeted him with these words: "You replace Dr. Franklin, I hear."

Jefferson responded, "Sir, I succeed Dr. Franklin; no one can replace him."

It was a great tribute to a great man, from a great man.

In 1790, Jefferson became our first Secretary of State. Alexander Hamilton was Secretary of the Treasury and the two differed on almost every issue. Each had his admirers and followers and from this early division of opinion developed our party system.

Jefferson resigned from the Cabinet in 1793 but was called back into public life in 1797 with his election to the vice presidency. Four years later he became the third president of the United States.

The new executive had little use for formality and ceremony, insisting upon simplicity at all times. He would allow no fuss or fanfare for his inauguration, but came to Washington as a private citizen and lodged overnight in a tavern. Just before noon on March 4th, he walked up Capitol Hill accompanied by a group of friends and quietly took the oath of office.

Greatest of all Jefferson's acts as president was undoubtedly his purchase of the Louisiana Territory from France for fifteen million dollars. Besides doubling the size of the country, the purchase threw the Mississippi River open to commercial traffic. This was very important, for there were no railroads and few wagon trails through the wilderness. People living on the Mississippi and all its tributaries now had a way to ship furs, lumber and other goods to New Orleans and on to the east coast and Europe.

Jefferson's second term as president began with a war against the pirates from the Barbary coast of Africa, who were raiding American ships. The war's successful outcome greatly strengthened our international position.

Several years later American commerce was again threatened when France tried to stop our trading with England, and England, our trading with France. Jefferson put through an Embargo Act, forbidding American ships to leave port. By this action he hoped to force England and France to yield to our wishes. However, American merchants raised such a protest, the Embargo was quickly repealed. Jefferson always claimed the War of 1812 could have been prevented had the act been enforced.

Retiring to Monticello in 1809, Jefferson planned to live there quietly alone, but the world soon beat a path to his door. Indeed, the demands on his hospitality were so great that he eventually found himself without money and in danger of losing his beloved home. When the news got about, however, the American public, eager to help the venerable man, sent large gifts of money to him.

Thomas Jefferson died July 4, 1826, exactly fifty years after the signing of the Declaration of Independence. He rests in the family burying grounds on his Monticello estate, where the epitaph he himself prepared may still be read:

"Here is buried Thomas Jefferson, author of the Declaration of Independence, of the Statute of Virginia for Religious Freedom, and Father of the University of Virginia."

Lou Gehrig

The Iron Horse of Baseball

IN FEW other lands is good sportsmanship respected and appreciated quite as much as it is in America. Lou Gehrig knew the true meaning of the phrase. He lived and died a graceful winner and a good loser. The astonishing record he established during his fourteen years as first baseman on the Yankee team made him a hero to millions of baseball fans. The quiet courage and great fortitude he displayed during the last two years of his life made him a hero to the entire nation.

Lou Gehrig was born June 19, 1903, in Upper Manhattan, New York. His parents, who had come to America from Germany just a few years before, named him Henry Louis, but he was always "Lou" to the public.

Three other Gehrig children had died as babies so all the hopes and ambitions of this honest, hard-working couple were centered in blond, dimple-cheeked Lou.

The boy received the usual public school education, doing well in his studies and playing soft ball and other games during recess and after school. In order to realize their ambitions for Lou's college education, his parents took jobs in a fraternity house at Columbia—his mother as cook and his father as man of all work. Saturdays, Lou was usually around the fraternity. There he would play ball with the college students, who called him "Heinie" and had a great affection for the rather shy, reserved boy.

As he grew older, Lou participated in more and more sports —baseball, football, basketball, skating and swimming. His parents did not like to see him spending so much time at games but as long as his grades in school were good, Lou was able to overcome their objections.

At New York High School of Commerce, the baseball coach soon realized that Lou had the makings of a real "slugger." Lou proved he was right. In 1920 when Commerce played Lane Tech for the Chicago-New York intercity championship at Wrigley Field, the handsome New Yorker provided fans with an unexpected thrill by hitting a homer over the right-field fence—a feat any big-league player would be proud of.

The next year Lou enrolled in the engineering school at Columbia. He went out for football and baseball, making both teams. Then one spring afternoon, in his sophomore year, Lou picked up a bat, stepped to the plate and with a tremendous swing of his powerful arms sent the ball sailing over center field. There was a roar from the bleachers and a gasp from both the dugout and pressbox. The ball finally came down four hundred feet from home plate—the longest home run ever hit by a

Lou Gehrig Became a Hero of Millions of Baseball Fans

member of any Columbia team.

Lou had hit himself right out of college. Scouts from professional teams were soon on his trail. His mother tearfully protested that baseball players were "bummers" but Lou knew that whether or not a man is a bum depends on himself, not on his business or profession. Giving up school, he signed with the Yankees.

During 1923 and 1924 Gehrig was farmed out to the Hartford, Connecticut team, but in 1925 he was assigned to cover first base for the Yankees.

In the next fourteen years Gehrig established one of baseball's most remarkable records. He played 2,130 consecutive major-league games with a batting average of .341. He topped the American League five times in runs scored, four times in total base hits and five times in home runs. He played in seven World Series and twice received the American League Most Valuable Player Award.

Nothing could keep Lou away 'from the diamond. He might break a finger or toe, he might be shaking with chills, but still he'd be there, playing as well as ever. In one game he was hit in the head with a ball and knocked unconscious. "Concussion" was the doctor's diagnosis, but Lou was back in the lineup the very next day. Is it any wonder the sports writers called him "The Iron Horse?"

The writers all liked Lou and among themselves called him kiddingly affectionate names, like "Old Piano Legs" and "Biscuit Pants."

As for the fans—they fairly idolized him, and Lou never let them down. When the kids asked for autographs he gave them good-naturedly. When older people crowded about him in public he was always polite, though he much preferred to be left alone.

Lou's personal habits were excellent. During off season, he

kept fit by walking, skating and deep-sea fishing. He always ate sensibly and got plenty of sleep. He never used alcohol or tobacco.

During spring training in 1939, Gehrig realized he wasn't nearly as fast as usual. He started forcing himself harder than ever but, soon after the season began, he knew something was definitely wrong. Early in May he benched himself, refusing to be a drag on his team.

After a thorough physical checkup, Gehrig was told that he was suffering from an unusual form of paralysis with no known cure. Lou accepted the diagnosis quietly. His great concern was to keep his parents and wife from knowing that the disease must eventually result in death.

But if Lou was made of hero's stuff, so was his wife. She knew even more than he. She knew that he had only two years to live. Yet on his arrival home from the clinic, she put on a gallant smile and never allowed anyone to tell him how short his time really was.

On July 4, 1939, Gehrig said good-by to the baseball world. The occasion was Lou Gehrig Appreciation Day—one of the most touching demonstrations of admiration and love ever accorded any American. The stands at Yankee stadium were jammed with more than sixty thousand friends and fans. Down on the diamond was the Postmaster General of the United States, the mayor of New York, members of Yankee teams for many years back—all gathered to take part in this tribute to a great ball player who was also a great and courageous man. Modest Lou was overwhelmed. With tears in his eyes he told the crowd, "For the past two weeks you have been reading about a bad break I got. Yet today I consider myself the luckiest man on the face of the earth . . ."

Shortly afterward Mayor La Guardia asked him to accept appointment as a New York City parole commissioner. Gehrig took three months to visit jails and study psychology, crime reports and the like. Once he was sure he could do the work well, he accepted. He continued as parole commissioner until the paralysis was so far advanced that he could not even feed himself without help.

On June 2, 1941, when it was announced that Lou Gehrig died at his home in New York with his devoted wife at his side, every flag in every ball park in America hung at half mast.

Silver-Tongued Statesman

No AMERICAN boy or girl needs to be told that Daniel Webster was one of our greatest orators. Americans know that as well as they know that George Washington was our first president. Webster's fame endured not only because of *what* he said but *how* he said it. His melodious voice, his magnetic personality and his striking appearance all combined to make him a man no listener could quickly forget.

From a humble beginning Webster literally talked his way into high places. When he spoke, all the world stopped to listen to his words. When he supported a cause, the cause was usually won.

During his life he gained fame, money and social recognition but the one thing he wanted most of all—the presidency of the United States—he never achieved.

Daniel Webster was born January 18, 1782, in Salisbury (now Franklin), New Hampshire. He was the youngest son of Ebenezer Webster, a farmer who held a respected place in the community and later became a judge.

The Websters were very poor. All the rest of the children had regular chores to do, but Daniel's health was frail and so he was seldom asked to do any heavy work. Instead, his father encouraged him in his love of reading. Ebenezer Webster had great respect for education.

The Constitution of the United States was drawn up in Philadelphia when Daniel was five years old. Not long afterward the stores were selling handkerchiefs on which the document was printed. One of these was given to little black-eyed Daniel and he soon had learned every word by heart.

At fourteen Daniel was sent to Phillips Exeter Academy. There the boy was unhappily selfconscious because of his poorly fitting homespun clothes. However, he studied hard and did very well in every subject but one. He failed miserably in speech!

After nine months at Exeter, Daniel taught school for a short time and with help from his father managed to scrape together enough money to enter Dartmouth College. He enrolled in 1797.

On arrival at Dartmouth, Daniel was still wearing homespun, but it didn't take him long to adopt the customs and costumes of his more fashionably dressed classmates. Before his four years were over he had become quite a dude or "macaroni" as they said in the eighteenth century.

At college his dark skin and hair won him the nickname of "Black Dan." He made many friends, read a great deal, and having lost his earlier shyness, soon became Dartmouth's best speaker and debater.

Following graduation, young Webster taught school at Fryeburg, Maine, and also worked evenings copying records. His teaching salary, $350 a year, was more than ample to pay his expenses, but he needed extra money to help his brother Ezekiel who was now in college. "Zeke" was always Daniel's favorite.

Later, young Webster went to Boston where he studied law in the office of Christopher Gore, a prominent lawyer. During this time he was offered a position as clerk in a New Hampshire county court but Gore influenced him to refuse the position and continue his studies. Old Ebenezer Webster was certain his son would never amount to anything, turning down opportunities like that!

Webster was admitted to the bar in 1805 and, after a brief period in Boscawen, set up a law office in Portsmouth. It wasn't long before his fame had spread throughout New Hampshire. Whenever he was present, the courtroom overflowed with visitors and he was much in demand for public addresses.

In 1812 Webster was elected to the national House of Representatives and served until 1817. Refusing re-election, he moved to Boston.

Subsequently, as a result of his brilliant defense in the Dartmouth College Case, decided by the Supreme Court, he was hailed as the country's foremost orator. His income soared and, in a few years' time, he was making well over ten thousand dollars a year.

Webster returned to the House of Representatives in 1823 and four years later was elected to the Senate. He began to think hopefully of the presidency. A short time before, when New Englanders had shifted their investments from shipping to manufacturing, he had abandoned support of free trade in favor of the protective tariff. He also shifted from state's rights to support of a strong central government. His oratory did not suffer with either change of attitude. He spoke as convincingly as ever.

During his life Webster made many great speeches, but none is more frequently quoted than his second "Reply to Hayne," delivered in 1830. Senator Hayne of South Carolina supported his state in her rebellious stand on a newly passed tariff law. Webster took the other side and during the course of the debate delivered the line you have heard so often: "Liberty and Union, now and forever, one and inseparable."

With the exception of two years as Secretary of State, Webster continued as Senator until 1850. In that year California asked admission to the Union as a free state. The South objected. To cover this and other disagreements regarding slavery, Henry Clay of Kentucky introduced his famous Compromise bill. Under it California would be admitted as a free state but a stricter law for the return of runaway slaves would also be enacted.

Persuaded that war would result if the Compromise were rejected, Webster spoke in its support, again emphasizing the importance of preserving the Union.

Clay's bill passed and it has often been said that without Webster's speech Civil War would have come eleven years sooner than it did. However, the speech cost Webster many of his Northern friends who could not stomach a stronger Fugitive Slave Law.

Shortly afterward, Webster became Secretary of State in President Fillmore's cabinet. Then came the election year, 1852. Twice before Webster's name had been among the Whig presidential candidates. This time he was confident of the nomination. Had he not gained many new friends in the South? But by the time the Whig convention was over Webster was a heartsick, disillusioned man. The South had not given him a single vote. Only his own faithful New England had stood behind him. The nomination had gone to General Scott.

Crushed in spirit, Webster returned to his beloved seaside home at Marshfield, Massachusetts. For years he had not been really well. Now his health failed rapidly. A few days before he died he asked that the American flag be flown day and night on his boat anchored in a cove below his bedroom window. A lighted lamp was also hung from the mast. Thus, with his flag in sight to the very last, Daniel Webster died on October 24, 1852.

Robert E. Lee

Hero of the Confederacy

MANY BELIEVE that Robert E. Lee was the greatest general of the Civil War. Certainly he was a brilliant leader and gracious gentleman, idolized by his own Confederate troops, respected by the Union troops.

At the outbreak of the war, Lee, then a colonel in the United States Army, was offered command of the Federal forces. He had freed his own slaves, he was against breaking up the Union, but he could not consider leading a war against his own homeland. Heavyhearted, he resigned his commission and offered his services to his own state, Virginia.

Robert Edward Lee belonged to the aristocracy of the South. Third son of Henry Lee, he was born on January 19, 1807, in the manor house of a large estate known as Stratford, located in Westmoreland County, Virginia. His father was the popular "Light Horse Harry" Lee, hero of the Revolutionary War, who had also served as governor of the State of Virginia. His mother was Anne Carter, member of another fine Virginia family. Two of his ancestors were among the signers of the Declaration of Independence.

Robert enjoyed the active outdoor life of the big plantation. When still a youngster, he was given a horse of his own and soon rode as though born in the saddle.

As the boy grew older, the family spent more and more time in Alexandria so that he might attend school there. He was an excellent student, courteous, sedate and friendly. His school-mates liked him as well as his teachers did, and he was a favorite companion for many sports, including hunting. At sixteen, Robert could shoot as well as he could ride.

Mrs. Lee was an invalid and to keep her happy, the youth would save up amusing little stories to tell her, accompany her on drives and do all sorts of thoughtful things.

At eighteen, Lee received an appointment to West Point Military Academy. It was a proud and happy moment for the young man who had always wanted to follow in his father's footsteps. His only regret was that his father could not be there to share his happiness. "Light Horse Harry" Lee had died seven years before.

At West Point, Lee made an almost perfect record. He studied hard, never received a demerit mark and graduated second in his class.

Entering the army as a second lieutenant, he was assigned to the engineering corps. Two years later he married Mary Custis, a great-granddaughter of Martha Washington.

The Custis family were wealthy landowners and Mary brought her husband a rich dowry, including the beautiful Lee home on the Potomac, now a national memorial and the site of Arlington National Cemetery.

During the years that followed, Lee served in many parts of the United States, always giving a good account of himself. He played an important part in the seige of Vera Cruz during the Mexican War, was superintendent of West Point for three years and in 1855 went to Texas as lieutenant colonel of a cavalry regiment.

Home on furlough four years later, Lee received orders to arrest John Brown, antislavery agitator who had seized the United States arsenal at Harper's Ferry. Lee did his duty and turned Brown over to the authorities but never had anything to say one way or the other about the affair.

Less than a month after being made a full colonel, the popular officer found himself faced with the unhappy problem of choosing between the North and the South. For two long days he shut himself away from the world, weighing every consideration. When his mind was finally made up, he never wavered. He would fight as hard and well for the Confederate States as he had always fought for the United States.

Needless to say, Jefferson Davis, president of the Confederacy, was glad Lee decided as he did. Davis made him his military adviser and later gave him command of the Army of Northern Virginia.

With Lee in charge, one success followed another. Even when his forces were greatly outnumbered the Southern general was usually able to hold his own. He was a master of strategy, but more than this, he was a master of men. The wholehearted devotion of his poorly equipped, often hungry troops seemed to give them unconquerable strength and spirit. Just the sight of their gray-uniformed leader was enough to set them cheering.

Stonewall Jackson, himself a great general, was Lee's second in command. Together they surprised the Union forces at Chancellorsville in May, 1863. After two days' fighting, Jackson rode out at twilight to inspect their position. In the uncertain light he was killed by one of his own men. Lee felt this loss keenly.

Following victory at Chancellorsville, Lee suffered defeat at Gettysburg, but in 1864 with sixty thousand men he fought Grant's army of more than one hundred thousand to a standstill in the famous Wilderness Campaign.

By the winter of 1864-65, however, the South had been considerably weakened, while the North was steadily gaining in strength. In February, Lee was made commander in chief of all the Confederate armies in the field, but by then it was evident that the Union forces must eventually win.

On April 9, 1865, after hard fighting, Lee was surrounded at Appomattox Court House, Virginia, and was forced to surrender to General Grant.

Two great men met that day to discuss peace terms. Lee's calm dignity did not forsake him in disaster, and Grant, with great understanding, did not ask for his sword, as was the custom.

Shortly afterward, Lee was pardoned for his part in the Civil War and the last years of his life were spent as president of Washington College in Lexington, Virginia. The institution prospered under the management of the efficient and gracious man who continued to be the idol of the South. In his honor, the name of the school was later changed to Washington and Lee University.

Robert E. Lee died in Lexington on October 12, 1870, admired and respected by all the nation.

American Naval Hero

ONE OF the most important naval engagements of the War of 1812 took place on September 10, 1813, when Lieutenant Oliver Hazard Perry scored a resounding victory over the British in the Battle of Lake Erie. Displaying a do-or-die spirit, he turned defeat into victory. His achievement gave the British a new respect for the United States and helped hasten the end of the war.

Son of Christopher and Sara Alexander Perry, Oliver Hazard Perry was born in South Kingston, Rhode Island, where his great-great-great-grandfather had settled in 1650. His father was a sea captain.

The sea fascinated the boy, too, and when he was fourteen he asked his father's permission to enter the Navy. Captain Perry was pleased with his son's request. He had just been given command of a new American frigate and helped arrange for

Oliver's appointment as midshipman on his ship.

The young midshipman in his handsome uniform was the envy of all his friends. His brothers and sisters spoke proudly of their "big brother in the Navy." Oliver's father was proud of him, for the boy did his work unusually well.

By 1812, Oliver had risen to the rank of lieutenant. That year war broke out between the United States and England. Much of the important fighting was done at sea and the rest of the world felt sure the big English navy would quickly wipe out the Amercian sea forces. But America sprang one surprise after another with victories at sea.

On land, however, things were not going well. The whole territory of Michigan had been taken by the British, with Indian help, and was protected by a strong British naval force on the Great Lakes.

The key to the situation was Lake Erie. If the Americans could gain control of this great body of water they would have Detroit and could probably retake all Michigan.

In February, 1813, Perry was given the job of clearing the British from Lake Erie. He was also given full responsibility for building a fleet on the spot to do the job.

This meant transporting hundreds of men and masses of supplies and materials from the Atlantic shore to Lake Erie. And at that time western New York and Pennsylvania were nothing but wilderness, full of unfriendly Indians. The few trails were narrow, rough and covered with snow.

It was a tremendous job, but Perry went calmly to work. By April construction was well under way at the port of Erie. By the middle of the summer his fleet of nine vessels was built.

Perry named his flagship the *Lawrence,* after Captain James Lawrence, who had been fatally wounded only a month or so before during a fierce Atlantic sea battle.

Perry established a base for his ships in the harbor of Put in

Bay, an island in the southwest end of Lake Erie. The British were sighted on September tenth, and Perry set out at once to meet them.

As they sailed to battle there was an unusual flag flying from the mast of the *Lawrence* below the Stars and Stripes. Its background was blue, and as the wind spread it wide, everyone aboard could read in large white letters Captain Lawrence's last inspiring words to his men: "Don't give up the ship!"

Officers and men were tense with anticipation. The distance between the *Lawrence* and the English squadron was rapidly closing. Two miles. A mile and a half. One mile. Then with a deafening roar, the British cannon opened fire. Carrying shorter range guns, the *Lawrence* was obliged to move in closer to return the fire. Soon the whole British squadron had her in range. The wind had died down, delaying the rest of the American ships. It was one ship against six and although the *Lawrence* fought valiantly, she could not overcome such odds. Before the other American ships could join the battle all but a handful of her men had been killed or wounded and it seemed a miracle that she even remained afloat.

Perry was determined to continue the fight from another ship. Taking five of his men, he started to cross to the *U.S.S. Niagara* in a rowboat. Smoke from the guns shrouded the lake, and it was a few minutes before a British lookout spotted the little boat. A shell plowed through its side. Quick as a flash Perry pulled off his coat and used it to plug the gaping hole.

Safely aboard the *Niagara* at last, Perry hoisted the blue and white flag from the *Lawrence* and renewed the fight. All the American vessels were now in the battle area. Following Perry's lead, each poured broadside after broadside into the British ships. The thunder of cannon was heard for miles, and the British soon realized they were beaten. In half an hour Perry returned to his flagship, *Lawrence* where he received the enemy's formal surrender.

Then General Harrison, the American commander, had to be notified at once. Not even waiting to go below, Perry wrote one of the most famous of all American naval dispatches on the back of an envelope:

"We have met the enemy and they are ours. Two ships, two brigs, one schooner and one sloop. Yours, with very great respect and esteem, O. H. Perry."

With Lake Erie won, the Michigan territory was soon regained and great progress was made toward ending the war.

Hailed a hero, Perry was promoted to captain, then the Navy's highest rank. He was also awarded a special gold medal by Congress.

Early in 1819, Perry was sent to Venezuela on a special government mission. He traveled as far as the mouth of the Orinoco river on a sloop, transferring to a schooner for the journey upstream to Angostura, then Venezuela's capital.

Seldom had Perry seen more beautiful country than that along the tropical river. But the heat was terrific and there seemed to be millions of mosquitoes.

Soon one after another of the men fell ill of yellow fever. No one knew at that time that the dread disease had any connection with the mosquitoes. It wasn't until eighty years later that Dr. Walter Reed proved that yellow fever is carried by just such mosquitoes as then swarmed along the Orinoco.

Captain Perry had just begun the voyage home when he awoke one morning with a severe chill. By the end of the day it was evident that he, too, had yellow fever. He was given every care, but his condition grew steadily worse. On his thirty-fourth birthday, August 23, 1819, Captain Oliver Hazard Perry died at sea. He was buried the following day on the island of Trinidad. Later a United States warship brought his body back to his own country for burial at Newport, Rhode Island.

America's Troubadour

THERE WAS a great deal of excitement the day Stephen Collins Foster was born in the little town of Lawrenceville, near Pittsburgh, Pennsylvannia. Bands played, people sang, important men made speeches. But it wasn't William and Eliza Foster's new little baby who caused the great celebration—it was the day on which he happened to be born: July 4, 1826, the fiftieth birthday of the United States.

One afternoon when Stephen was seven, he and his mother were in a music store. Browsing about, little Stevie came upon a flageolet, which is a shrill little wooden flute. He had never seen one before but in a short time he was playing *Hail, Columbia* so the tune could be recognized. Not long after this he was given a flute and taught himself to play it very well. Later he taught himself to play the piano, too.

Stephen never had any real music lessons. His parents realized he had musical talent, but they did not think music a suitable profession for a man.

One of the most exciting happenings in Stephen's childhood was a trip he made down the Ohio river with his mother and an older sister. When the boat stopped at Augusta, Kentucky, the Fosters got off to visit two of Stephen's uncles. Here the boy saw Negro slaves for the first time. After two weeks or so they went on to Louisville. They also visited Cincinnati, then known as "the Queen City of the West."

When it came time to go to school, Stephen didn't mind studying, but he felt "cooped up" in a classroom. He often played hookey and went down to the wharves along the river. There he played his flute and listened to the Negro laborers sing at their work. The Fosters worried about what they were to do with this boy whose only real interest was music.

During the winter of 1840, Stephen was sent to an academy in Athens, Pennsylvania. For years his head had been full of music and he had made up many little pieces to play on his flute. At Athens he wrote down one of these compositions for the first time. He called it the "Tioga Waltz."

Stephen was unhappy at the academy because he was homesick. He stayed only a year. After a few weeks at another school, he remained at home, studying French, German and mathematics with a private tutor.

When Stephen was sixteen he had his first song published. The song was called "Open Thy Lattice, Love" and he dedicated it to ten-year-old Susan Pentland who lived next door. Stephen wrote the music. The words were from a poem by an English writer.

A couple of years later Stephen helped form a singing club called "The Knights of the S.T." None of the members told what the mysterious "S.T." stood for, though friends guessed it meant "Square Table."

One night Stephen surprised the Knights with a new Negro song—one he had written himself. He called it "Louisiana Belle." The following week he wrote another called "Old Uncle Ned." The boys sang these songs wherever they went and soon all Pittsburgh knew them.

The year Stephen was twenty, he was sent to Cincinnati to work as a bookkeeper. Stephen did his work well, but music was still his greatest joy. One day he took three of his songs to a music publisher. The songs were "Louisiana Belle," "Old Uncle Ned" and a new one, called "Oh! Susanna." The publisher said he would print them all. It didn't occur to Stephen to ask for payment. All he wanted was to see his songs in print. So he was delighted when the publisher paid him one hundred dollars for "Oh! Susanna." He did not realize it was worth far more. His only payment for the other songs was a few free copies.

During the big California gold rush "Oh! Susanna" became a sort of theme song for the thousands of people hurrying West. Soon it was being sung clear across the continent.

Stephen sold more songs—many of them to owners of important minstrel troupes like E. P. Christy. After three years, he gave up his bookkeeping job to return home and start writing songs in earnest. These he sold on a royalty basis, getting a certain amount on each copy sold.

Probably the most famous of all Foster's songs is the one entitled "The Old Folks at Home." He had had the new song on his mind for several days when he dropped in to see his brother Morrison one morning.

"Can you think of a southern river with a two syllable name?" Stephen asked.

Morrison suggested the Pee Dee River but Stephen said he had already thought of that. He wanted something different.

His brother then brought out a map of the southern states. As they studied it together, Stephen's eyes suddenly lit on a little river in Florida. "The Suwannee! That's just what I want. Thanks!" And off he went to finish the song. Although it's title is "The Old Folks at Home," most people call it "Swanee River," since it begins, "Way down upon de Swanee ribber."

When Stephen showed this song to Christy, the minstrel liked it so well he wanted to introduce it as one of his own. So Stephen sold Christy the right to sing it before it was published and the right to say he was the composer. It wasn't generally known until years later that Stephen had written this song, which was extraordinarily popular from its first performance.

Stephen fell in love shortly after his return home from Cincinnati. The girl was lovely Jane McDowell. He had known her a long time but had always thought of her only as a friend. When Stephen went to call on Jane, the door was often opened by a kindly old colored servant. The old man's name was Joe and he always had a big smile for Stephen. One night the composer told him he was going to "put him in a song." He did, too, but it wasn't until long afterward. "Old Black Joe" was the last Negro song Foster wrote.

Stephen and Jane were married and were very happy for several years. Then problems arose that they could not always solve and they separated several times. During one of these separations Stephen poured out his love and loneliness in one of his greatest songs, "Jeannie With the Light Brown Hair."

Finally, because they needed money, Jane decided to go to work. It was very unusual for a married woman to work outside of her home in those days. Stephen went alone to New York where they had lived for several years. He became very dejected. Though he wrote many songs, he sold most of them for very little. He lived in a shabby room. He seldom ate a regular meal. He drank a great deal and soon lost all interest in life.

On a wintry January day in 1864, George Cooper, one of

Foster's friends, found the song-writer lying ill in his room. He had fallen with a water pitcher and cut himself badly. Stephen was taken to a hospital, but it was too late. On January 13, 1864, America's best-loved composer died.

During his short life, Stephen Foster had written about one hundred seventy-five songs, many of which will never be forgotten, but when he died he had only thirty-eight cents in his pocket. Along with the money was a fragment of paper bearing the words, "Dear friends and gentle hearts." It may be that he had been about to write another of his tender and beautiful songs.

Ethan Allen

Leader of the Green Mountain Boys

As LEADER of the Green Mountain Boys in their history-making attack on Fort Ticonderoga, Ethan Allen earned undying fame for himself throughout America. In addition, Vermonters honor him as their state's staunchest champion in colonial days.

It was on May 10, 1775, that Allen surprised the British at Ticonderoga in the first offensive action of the Revolutionary War. His Green Mountain Boys were mainly woodsmen and farmers, without any regular military training; and while they were excellent shots, their guns were old-fashioned and slow to load and fire. A few men had only swords or clubs with which to fight.

But they took the fort—and took it without a single casualty. Except for sentries, the British were all asleep as Allen and his

Boys swarmed into the fort at dawn.

In the lead, Allen quickly sprang to the stair of the officers' quarters. Roaring like a lion, he ordered the commander to come out at once. An astonished Britisher appeared without delay, but since he had had no time to dress, he was forced to make this historic appearance with his breeches over his arm. He demanded to know by what authority Allen entered the fort.

"In the name of the Great Jehovah and the Continental Congress," shouted Ethan Allen, so it is claimed.

These dramatic words, now famous, got results. The fort surrendered and within hours the garrison at Crown Point had fallen. A British sloop of war at Fort St. John was also taken.

It is true that the British had less than fifty men at Fort Ticonderoga, but they were trained troops, and at the time of attack only eighty-three of Allen's two hundred and thirty men were at the fort, because of the difficulty in getting boats to cross Lake Champlain.

In attacking, Allen had only the questionable authority of the Connecticut Committee of Correspondence, an anti-British group of colonials, but the Continental Congress later authorized pay for all who had taken part.

Ethan Allen was born on January 10, 1737, in Litchfield, Connecticut, the son of Joseph and Mary Allen. He worked hard as a boy and with his hunting, fishing and trapping helped provide food for the table and animal skins for the family's clothing. He learned to read and write when very young and read every book he could lay hands on.

He was a giantlike man both in size and strength. Using only his teeth he could pick up a large bag of salt and fling it over his shoulder. People said he once strangled a bobcat with his hands and that he was able to bite heavy nails into bits.

The Green Mountain Boys were organized during a period of bitter quarreling between the colonies of New York and New

Hampshire. Both colonies claimed the area which is now Vermont and both sold land in this area, with the result that two different buyers often claimed the same section. Soon all those who had bought from New Hampshire were banded together against those who had bought from New York, with Allen leader of the New Hampshire group.

There were quite a few fights, and when the governor of New York swore he was going to chase Allen and his followers "clear across Vermont and into the Green Mountains," they started calling themselves "The Green Mountain Boys." The name stuck.

The secret signal of the Boys was a hoot like an owl's, and when Allen led them into action he would start off with the shout, "We're going on a big wolf hunt!"

In 1771 Allen was declared an outlaw by the New York governor, but after the fall of Fort Ticonderoga a truce was declared and the Green Mountain Boys were admitted to the New York Provincial militia, on the recommendation of Congress.

Serving under General Schuyler, Allen was sent to Canada to win Indians and Canadians over to the colonial cause. He had rounded up one hundred and ten when he met Major John Brown, also of the Continental Army, who persuaded him to join in an attack on Montreal.

Allen did his part, but Brown failed to show up and the big Vermonter was taken prisoner.

Two unhappy years of captivity followed. Allen was not well treated and the only bright spot came when a group of sympathetic Irish showered him with an assortment of handsome clothing. He was finally freed in an exchange of prisoners.

Trouble was soon renewed between Vermont and New York. Vermont declared itself an independent republic. A militia was established and Allen was made a brigadier general. With other leaders he worked unceasingly for the admission of Vermont to the Union as an independent state. In this connection he had some dealings with the British, apparently suggesting that Vermont might become a province of Canada if Congress refused recognition. Because of this a charge of treason was brought, which was never verified.

Ethan Allen died near Burlington, Vermont, on February 13, 1789, and was given a military funeral. Two years later his most cherished dream was realized—Vermont became the fourteenth state in the Union.

America's First Man of Letters

WASHINGTON IRVING was a friendly man. He liked people and people liked him. This genial fellow gave our country laughter—a very important contribution indeed. Life had been all too serious during the new republic's first difficult years. Americans needed to laugh and to see the amusing side of their life.

Writing skillfully and sympathetically, Irving highlighted the humorous aspects of life in America. He also wrote many serious things, but it was his humorous writing which won him his first fame and which has proved most enduring.

Washington Irving was born in New York on April 3, 1783. He was the youngest of the eleven children of Deacon William Irving who was a Revolutionary patriot and a successful merchant.

The Irvings lived on William Street, then part of the city's

residential district, and here Washington spent a happy childhood. He was sent to school when he was four, but it soon became evident that Washington did not like to study. He read
far more than the other children, but unless his mother kept
after him every minute he paid little attention to his other subjects.

New York's city hall, Capitol of the United States in 1789,
was not far from the Irving home and there the boy saw George
Washington, for whom he was named, inaugurated as our first
president. Shortly after the inaugural the Irvings' maid glimpsed
the President in the neighborhood. Grasping little Washington
by the hand, the girl led him over to the great man and announced respectfully that the child was a namesake of his. President Washington smilingly patted the little fellow on the head
and gave him his blessing. Irving never forgot the incident.

As he grew to manhood, he enjoyed the bustling life of New
York. His charming personality opened all doors to him. Every
day brought invitations to the city's finest social functions.
Though not politically minded himself, he made friends with
many of the nation's lawmakers and statesmen. He tramped
along Broadway, then a country road, with a gun on his shoulder, and shot squirrels in the woods along the Hudson river. He
mingled with the theatrical celebrities of the day. He dabbled
in drawing, enjoyed music and admired art. His whole manner
of living was a reflection of the artistic and cultural growth of
this new city.

About 1800 he began studying law and was admitted to the
bar in 1806, but he was never very serious in either the study or
the practice of his profession.

As a youth of eighteen, Irving fell in love with Matilda Hoff-
man, the daughter of a lawyer. Matilda was a lovely and intelligent girl, and the two were admirably suited to each other.
Then, tragically, Matilda died when only seventeen. Irving was

inconsolable. He later became one of New York's gayest "men about town," but never forgetting Matilda, remained a bachelor all his life.

In 1803, Matilda's father and Irving made a trip by oxcart and scow through upper New York to Montreal. It was a rough, hard trip and most of their nights were spent in wretched inns, but Irving took it all in his stride. He enjoyed every moment and came back eager to see more of the world.

The opportunity came sooner than he expected. Irving had never been robust. Now his health took a turn for the worse, and his family sent him to Europe. After two years of happy wandering, he returned, well again and more sought after than ever.

Realizing he would never make a lawyer, Irving turned to writing. His whimsical essays on the city's social life, books, theaters and politics gained him quite a reputation as a wit.

In 1809 appeared his first long work—the comic *Diedrich Knickerbocker's History of New York*. It was cleverly advertised in very serious tone, giving readers a great surprise when they found it to be a rollicking burlesque of New York's early Dutch settlers.

The success of this book should have inspired Irving to settle down to serious writing, but his family was wealthy and he drifted rather aimlessly for several years.

News of the burning of Washington, D.C., by the British in 1814 reached Irving aboard a Hudson river boat. As one passenger related the details, another made a sneering remark about James Madison, then President. Irving rebuked the fellow in no uncertain terms, concluding with the statement that every loyal citizen should be earnest to avenge this outrage. He immediately offered his services to his country and was made aide-de-camp to Governor Tompkins.

When the war was over, Irving sailed for England. There he

ran into financial difficulties and had to write to make a living. But he proved his mettle and did some of his finest work during the following years.

Then as now, his most popular work was *The Sketch Book of Geoffrey Crayon, Gent.* This work contains thirty-two stories and essays which include two of America's best-loved tales, *The Legend of Sleepy Hollow* and *Rip Van Winkle.* Though this book was published under the name of Crayon, it was generally known that Irving was the author.

The Van Tassels and their home on the Hudson play an important part in *The Legend of Sleepy Hollow.* This place really existed and in 1835, three years after his return to America, Irving bought it for his own home. He called it "Sunnyside" and spent some of his happiest years there. Becoming an amateur gardener, Irving raised a great variety of fruits and vegetables, boasting to his friends, with a twinkle in his eye, that the produce he raised cost him only a little more than twice as much as it would in the market!

From 1843 to 1846, Irving served his country as minister to Spain. He did well but was glad to return to Sunnyside.

His last long work was the five-volume biography, *A Life of George Washington.* This was a long, hard task, and Irving's death was perhaps hastened by his labors.

Washington Irving died of a heart attack on November 28, 1859, at the age of seventy-six years.

The Foxhole Reporter

MOST PEOPLE think of war correspondents as glamorous men and women who dash around with pad and pencil, talking with generals and writing important articles about military strategy.

Ernie Pyle, greatest of all World War II correspondents, wasn't anything like that. He often said he didn't know anything about strategy and tactics. It was the plain G.I.'s who were most important to Ernie. He was interested in everything they said and did, and he wanted the folks back home to know and appreciate what a great job the "doughfeet" were doing.

Ernie Pyle was often called "the foxhole reporter" because he went right up to the front lines to get his stories. He moved around among different outfits, staying with each for several days. He would eat and sleep with the enlisted men, sharing all their dangers, talking with them about home, the war, the future, everything they had on their minds. The only notes he made were of names and addresses. His dispatches were full of them, and he wanted to be sure they were right.

"I'm really a letter writer," Ernie Pyle once said. And that's what his stories always seemed to be—letters from the boys themselves, telling how they lived, what they ate, what they talked about. He wrote about how tired they were and how dirty—what it was like to sleep in a muddy foxhole. He made his readers feel the great sorrow of never-ending death. When something funny happened, he wrote about that, too, but to Ernie there was nothing funny in war itself. He hated and feared it. Right from the start he had a premonition of death, but he stayed on even though he didn't have to do so.

Ernie Pyle was born on a farm near Dana, Indiana, August 3, 1900. His parents, William and Maria Taylor Pyle named him Ernest Taylor Pyle and he was always "Ernest" to them.

Ernie's boyhood was like that of any farm youngster. He went to bed early and got up early. Nine months a year he went to school where the other kids called him "Shag." His hobby was collecting picture postcards. He didn't have any special ambition, but he was anxious to see the world.

After serving with the Navy in the first World War, the young veteran studied journalism at the University of Indiana. He said afterward that the only reason he took journalism was that he had heard it was an easy course.

Ernie was crazy about football, but he wasn't big enough to play. He never weighed more than one hundred fifteen pounds. However, he did get to be football manager and traveled with the team. One year the university baseball team made a trip to the Orient. Ernie got permission to go along and worked his way to Hongkong.

The LaPorte, Indiana, *Herald-Argus* gave Ernie his first newspaper job. He was a cub reporter. After a few months he left to work on the Washington, D. C., *News*.

On July 7, 1925, Pyle was married to Geraldine Siebolds. Mrs. Pyle liked to travel, too, and a year later they took their first long trip. They drove around the United States.

Five years later when Pyle was offered the job of roving reporter for the Scripps-Howard newspapers, he jumped at the chance. During the next five years he crossed the United States thirty-five times and went to Central and South America, Mexico, Canada, Alaska and the Hawaiian Islands. There wasn't often any big news in the daily columns he wrote, but people liked them a lot. They liked the way he described the things he saw and told what ordinary people everywhere were saying and thinking. They smiled at the way he always called his wife "That Girl."

Then in 1940, Pyle gave up his carefree touring to cover the first dreadful bombing of England by Germany. He was back in England again in 1942, traveling among the camps and writing stories about the American boys over there.

One day in October, 1942, Ernie received word to be ready to move. That's all he was told. Everything had to be kept secret to keep enemy spies from learning the Allies' plans. But that night he was sent aboard a British troop ship along with hundreds of American soldiers. Some of the soldiers had brought their pets along even though it was against the ship's regulations. One soldier slipped by all the inspection officers with two wriggling puppies hidden under his shirt.

This particular ship was one of a great convoy of troop and supply ships traveling together. Everyone was warned not to throw cigarette butts or scraps overboard as they would leave a trail for enemy submarines. Each ship was blacked out and there were strict orders against smoking on deck at night as the light of a single cigarette can be seen for miles at sea. After several days, it was announced that the convoy was to take part in the Allied invasion of Africa.

Not long after landing safely, Pyle was walking along a road in Africa when some German Stukas swooped down in a strafing attack. He jumped into a ditch beside an American soldier just as a shower of bullets hit the ground all around. When the planes were gone Pyle breathed a sigh of relief and said to the soldier, "Whew, that was close, wasn't it?" Getting no answer, he leaned over and discovered that the soldier, only a foot away, had been killed.

Pyle was greatly shaken by this experience. The next dispatch he wrote showed how deeply he felt about the unknown boy who had died beside him.

When the Allies went into Italy in the summer of 1943, Pyle went, too. There, during an early morning bombing of the Anzio beachhead, he had another narrow escape. Sleeping at press headquarters, he jumped from his bed to look out the window when the bombing began. Ordinarily this would have been the worst thing he could have done, but a second later two walls of the room were blown in and his bunk was buried under falling plaster and boards. Running to the window probably saved his life.

Pyle covered the Allies' triumphant march into Paris in 1944 but decided soon afterward that he must have a rest. He had seen so much death he was afraid he couldn't go on and stay sane. He said so in his columns and everyone liked him more than ever because of his frankness.

But after several months at his home in Albuquerque, New Mexico, with "That Girl" he was off again—this time to the Pacific front.

Early in April, Pyle landed with American troops on Okinawa. A few days later he went over to Ie, a tiny island near by. Just before going, he asked a friend who was returning home to tell his wife he would be home soon, too—this would be "his last landing.

But Ernie didn't get home. On April 18, 1945, he started for the front lines on Ie with a lieutenant colonel. They were riding along in a jeep when a Jap machine gunner opened fire. The two men dove into a ditch. A few minutes later the little correspondent raised his head to see if the coast was clear and was instantly killed as three bullets went through his helmet.

Ernie Pyle was buried on Ie among the men whose good friend he had been. A special statement commemorating the gallant writer was issued by President Truman as America's highest officials joined with millions of everyday Americans in mourning the death of the G.I.'s friend and champion.

Patrick Henry

The Voice of Freedom

BACK IN America's colonial days, before the Revolutionary War, thousands of people were dissatisfied with the rule of King George III of England. They frequently complained bitterly among themselves, but not until 1765 when Patrick Henry introduced his famous "Virginia Resolutions" denouncing the Stamp Act, did anyone have the courage to come out in open resistance against an act of the King. Patrick Henry was the first man in all the colonies to protest openly—and ten years later he was also the first to declare publicly, "We must fight!"

Each time he spoke out, he risked arrest on a charge of treason, and treason was punishable by death.

Yes, Patrick Henry was surely a courageous man, but even more important he was an orator without equal—the most persuasive speaker of his time. People didn't just listen to his words and forget—they did as he wanted them to. His persuasive powers were tremendous.

Yet early in his life, Patrick Henry had failed three times in attempts to make a living.

John Henry, Patrick's father, was a well-educated Scotsman who had come to America in the 1720's. His mother was of Welsh descent, noted for her conversational and musical talents and described as a "portly, handsome dame."

The Henrys had a small plantation in Hanover County, Virginia, and here Patrick was born on May 29, 1736.

Patrick attended school until he was about ten, then spent some time studying Latin, Greek, mathematics and history under his father and an uncle, who was rector of the parish.

Just how much he got from this schooling no one seems to know. In later years he liked to say that he was just an ignorant fellow without education, but he probably learned more at this time than he pretended.

In addition, Patrick Henry had a gift for learning through observation and conversation. When he saw something new, he studied it carefully. When he talked with a person who might contribute something to his knowledge, he drew that person out—led him to talk about the subjects on which he was an expert.

At fifteen, Patrick was put to work clerking in a store. The following year, he and his brother went into business for themselves, but their store failed within a year.

Meanwhile Patrick had fallen in love with Sarah Shelton and, although he had neither money nor job, they were married when he was eighteen.

As a dowry Sarah brought him three hundred acres of land and six slaves, so young Henry became a farmer. Then in 1757, when his home burned, he started another store. It lasted just two years.

Henry now decided to study law. Today it takes many years of study to become a lawyer, but this was not true in Henry's time. Many men received permits to practice law after only a few months' study. This was the case with Henry, but he soon showed unusual ability in the law.

At the end of two years he had enough clients to live comfortably and, during his third year of practice, he skyrocketed to prominence with the fiery eloquence he displayed during a case involving church taxes, known ; the "Parsons' Cause." After this, his business boomed and he became known as the friend of the common people.

In May, 1765, Patrick Henry was elected to fill a vacancy in the Virginia legislature. That same month, on his twenty-nin th birthday, he touched off the spark of public resistance that eventually led to the Revolutionary War.

As he rose to his feet, stoop-shouldered and rather gangly in his ill-fitting clothes, he must have looked far more like an ignorant farmer than a man a king should fear.

Then, to his listeners' shocked surprise, he read his history-making series of "Virginia Resolutions," saying in effect that "the general assembly of this colony have the only and sole exclusive right and power to lay taxes."

A furious debate followed during which Henry made his famous point: "Caesar had his Brutus; Charles the First his Cromwell; and George the Third—" (here he was interrupted by shouts of "Treason! Treason!" but he continued) "—may profit by their example. If this be treason, make the most of it!"

Voting was close, but the Resolutions were adopted, and soon other colonies followed Virginia's lead.

Patrick Henry had become the spokesman of the colonial cause, and the common people practically idolized him. "If Patrick Henry says so, it must be right," was the general feeling.

When making a speech, Henry was always solemn and usually dressed in black, but otherwise he was a good-natured, sociable fellow who liked to dance and play the fiddle. He was a great storyteller and often talked with a backwoods accent, although he could speak correctly when he wanted to.

His "we must fight" speech—the greatest of his great career—was made March 23, 1775. Throughout the speech his eloquence was at its peak. His gestures were even more dramatic than usual. His voice rose like thunder, and he finished with these thrilling words: "Is life so dear, or peace so sweet, as to be purchased at the price of chains and slavery? Forbid it, Almighty God! I know not what course others may take; but as for me, give me liberty, or give me death!"

The effect of these words on his audience was stupendous. One listener said he felt "ill with excitement." Another was so moved he asked to be buried at the spot where the fiery words were spoken.

A few weeks later the Revolutionary War began. Henry served for a time as a commander in chief of the Virginia troops, but gave up his commission early in 1776.

On July fourth of that year he signed the Declaration of Independence and the following day he was sworn in as Virginia's first governor.

During the next three years Henry lived quite differently from what he had in the past. His annual salary was one thousand pounds (about five thousand dollars) and he was also voted one thousand pounds for furniture for the governor's palace at Williamsburg. During this period, he put aside the simple clothes he usually wore and dressed in the height of fashion, as was expected of a governor.

After leaving office, Henry retired to his large estate in Henry County—but in 1784 was returned to Williamsburg as governor and served two one-year terms, refusing a third.

At the Virginia Convention of 1788, called to approve or reject the new Constitution, Patrick Henry led the opposition, believing the federal government had been given too much power at the states' expense. His objections were finally overruled, however, largely through Washington's influence, and Virginia voted for acceptance.

Patrick Henry was a member of the legislature until 1790. Four years later he gave up his law practice because of ill health, and though Washington later asked him first to serve as Secretary of State and then as Chief Justice of the Supreme Court, he was forced to refuse.

His last years were spent living quietly with his family at Red Hill, his home on the Staunton River. He died there June 6, 1799, shortly after he had been persuaded to run for the legislature of Virginia once more.

Eli Whitney

Inventor of the Cotton Gin

ELI WHITNEY had never even seen raw cotton seed until a few weeks before he invented the cotton gin. He was a New Englander and a newcomer to the South. He knew little about its problems, nor did he guess as he built his gin (short for "engine") what its far-reaching effects would be.

With the invention of the cotton gin, life in the South changed almost overnight. Hundreds of thousands of acres of land were planted in cotton. Shiploads of cotton lint were exported to Europe. Money poured into the cotton-raising states. Fortunes were made, and the whole section became important and wealthy.

But there were other results from Whitney's invention—much less happy results.

Before the cotton gin, slavery was on the verge of dying out

101

in the United States. Southern planters retained their slaves more through sentiment than anything else. The spurt in cotton production changed all that. Now there was a great demand for labor. By using slaves, who received no wages, profits were bigger. The anti-slave sentiment was stifled by greed. In this indirect way, the cotton gin was one of the causes of the Civil War.

As for Whitney, although his invention marked the birth of one of America's greatest industries, it brought him only sorrow and disappointment.

Eli Whitney was born at Westboro, Massachusetts, December 8, 1765, the son of Eli Whitney, Senior, a well-to-do farmer.

Young Eli showed little interest in his schoolwork, but when it came to puttering in his father's workshop—that was quite a different story! The boy was never happier than when building a birdhouse or taking a clock apart. When only twelve years old, he made a fiddle that people said possessed a very nice tone.

Three years later, he started a regular business of making nails by hand. The Revolutionary War had cut down imports of machine-made nails, and the demand for Eli's was great. After the war he made hatpins, canes and other small items.

During his early teens Eli had no desire to go to college, but later he wisely changed his mind. He decided that no matter what he might do for a living, an education would be helpful. From then on he carefully saved his money and, when twenty-three years old, entered Yale.

Following graduation in 1792, he left for Savannah, Georgia, to take a teaching position and during the trip down he made the acquaintance of General Nathanael Greene's widow, a gracious Southern lady. When the promised position came to nothing and Whitney expressed a desire to become a lawyer, Mrs. Greene invited him to live in her home while studying.

Young Whitney was glad to accept and, in return for her kindness, he made toys for her children and helped all he could around the house and plantation. Mrs. Greene was especially delighted when he made her a new embroidery frame, much better than any other she had.

One evening a group of planters came to visit Mrs. Greene. As they talked, the men expressed deep concern over the future of the South if nothing was done to better agricultural conditions. The soil seemed suitable only for raising cotton, but the expense of separating seed from lint was too great to make widespread planting worthwhile.

"Why, it takes a slave a whole day to remove the seed from a single pound," one of the visitors remarked. "There ought to be a faster way."

Mrs. Greene thought so, too, and suggested that Whitney might have some ideas. He quickly explained that he knew absolutely nothing about cotton, but promised to investigate.

The very next day he set to work and in a brief time he had constructed his first cotton gin. It was a simple machine turned by a crank, and with its help one man could remove the seeds from fifty pounds of cotton in a day. Fifty times more than before!

As news of the invention spread, people flocked to Savannah to see the machine for themselves. All were amazed that so difficult a problem could be solved with such a comparatively simple device.

With Phineas Miller as his partner, Whitney applied for patents and hurried to New Haven, Connecticut, to set up a manufacturing plant, never dreaming what difficulties lay ahead.

Before production even got started the factory burned down. Money had to be borrowed to build another and by the time it was finished, others were already marketing gins, using Whitney's ideas without permission. Forced to fight for his rights, one lawsuit followed another. Then cotton buyers in England said Whitney's gin was injuring the cotton fiber. Two years were spent in proving this untrue. Trouble piled on trouble until Miller finally died, a disappointed and broken man.

Fortunately, Whitney had had the foresight to start a second business, and in 1798 had received a government contract to make firearms. When finally convinced that his cotton gin would never gain him anything but misery, he gave his full time to his gun factory. Here he was the first manufacturer to introduce modern factory methods and made a great financial success.

Eli Whitney died in his home at New Haven, Connecticut, January 8, 1825, at the age of sixty years.

Knute Rockne

King of the Gridiron

ALTHOUGH THE young men that Knute Rockne so often led to gridiron glory were far from being all Irish, their spirit and driving power earned them the title of the "Fighting Irish." Likewise, even though America is no land for kings, no one has denied to the "Rock" of Notre Dame the right to the mythical crown in the kingdom of football.

Rockne was first of all a builder of men. Out of them he fashioned football teams that made history in the sport world.

The chunky, bald Norwegian was probably the greatest football coach of all time. Strangely enough, his ambition all through college was to be a chemist. Although his career as a coach was thrust upon him, he gave it everything he had.

Knute Kenneth Rockne was born in Voss, Norway, on March 4, 1888, son of Lars K. and Martha Gjermo Rockne. Knute was

105

the only son in a family of five children.

By the time he was four, little Knute was able to skate, ski and steer a sled. Before he was five he could swim, fish and ride a horse.

Lars Rockne was a stationary engineer and skilled woodworker. He built beautiful carriages as a hobby and in 1891 came to America to display a particularly fine one at the World's Fair in Chicago. Mr. Rockne liked America so well, he sent for his family and they settled in Chicago.

As a youngster Knute played baseball, but his parents forbade his playing football "because he might get hurt." Then one day Knute was hit in the nose with a baseball bat. His poor nose was practically flattened against his face, but Knute felt triumphant. Now surely his folks would see that football was no more dangerous than baseball! The boy won the argument and he played end on the high-school team.

Knute earned spending money by working Saturdays and vacations. He washed windows and ran errands, and one summer he worked on a Wisconsin farm.

Like all Scandinavians, Knute's father had great respect for education and was eager to see his son in college. However, when Knute was dropped from high school in his senior year, because of playing hookey to practice pole-vaulting, his father decided he should go to work.

For the next five years Knute worked in the Chicago post office. By 1910 he had saved a thousand dollars and decided to resume his education. He was thinking of entering the University of Illinois when two friends urged him to enter Notre Dame with them. "Who's ever heard of Notre Dame?" asked Rockne, but he finally decided to go.

At that time, football was a much rougher game than it is now. The forward pass was seldom used and weight was more important than speed. However, when Rockne was elected cap-

Rockne Experimented With the Forward Pass

tain of the 1913 Notre Dame team he and Charles E. Dorais, the quarterback, did some experimenting with the forward pass. When they put their system into play against West Point, Notre Dame won a sensational 35 to 13 victory. This awakened coaches to the possibilities offered by an "open game."

Rockne graduated from Notre Dame in 1914 with a scholastic average of 92.5. This is all the more exceptional when one knows that besides participating in several sports, he worked for his tuition and meals, edited the college annual one year, and was active in dramatics.

Following graduation Rockne returned to Notre Dame as chemistry instructor and assistant football coach. Four years later he became head coach.

During the next twelve years Rockne developed some of the finest football teams this country has ever seen. The success he achieved with a game based on shifting and passing is largely responsible for the faster, safer football we have today.

Between 1918 and 1930 the Fighting Irish compiled an amazing record. It consisted of one hundred and five victories, twelve defeats and five ties.

Besides vigorous workouts on the practice field, Rockne set up a strict program of everyday living for his teams: no smoking, nine hours sleep every night, no heavy pastries, meat once a day, and plenty of milk and fruit. He expected a lot of his men, but because he was always friendly and good-humored, they co-operated fully.

Rockne made frequent speeches, wrote articles on football and conducted a summer school for coaches. In March, 1931, he accepted an offer to supervise some motion picture shorts on football and decided to fly to California. On March 31, 1931, he was killed when his plane crashed in Kansas.

"Rock" is buried at Notre Dame where his name has become a legend with the students.

Hunter, Scout and Showman

BUFFALO BILL CODY was the last of the great scouts who helped blaze America's way westward. He was fearless, honest, reliable and decent—a man who could outride and outshoot anyone he ever met and who seemed to know the West by instinct. Even in new country he could find his way unerringly, locating water and the best camp sites as easily as if he had a map to guide him.

William Frederick Cody, son of Isaac Cody, was born on February 26, 1846, on a farm near Davenport, Iowa. When little Bill was eight, the family moved to Kansas, traveling west with three prairie schooners and a large carriage. Bill rode his pony all the way.

In Salt Creek Valley, where the Codys settled, Bill played with Indian children, learned their language, and became as expert with a bow and arrow as he was with a gun.

Bill's father made many enemies in Kansas because of his strong antislavery views. Once he was stabbed by one of these enemies. The wound never healed properly, and Mr. Cody died when Bill was only eleven years old.

Bill, now the family breadwinner, got a job with one of the big wagon trains that moved between the Mississippi and the Coast. Indian attacks were frequent and Bill soon learned that it was "kill or be killed."

At fourteen the boy became a rider for the Pony Express which carried mail between St. Joseph, Missouri, and Sacramento, California. At first he had a short run of forty-five miles. Later, he rode a seventy-five mile stretch. There were relay stations along the way, fifteen to twenty miles apart. At each of these, Bill stopped just long enough to get a fresh pony. Between stations he rode like the wind. At the end of his run he turned his mail pouch over to the next rider, picked up the east-bound mail and started back immediately. One time he rode his own stretch and the next rider's, too, without resting! The round trip totaled three hundred twenty-two miles.

During the Civil War Bill served several months as a Union spy. Wearing a Confederate uniform he ventured into the enemy camps and obtained much valuable information for the northern army. Later he was stationed at St. Louis where he met Louise Frederici. She became his wife in 1866.

Great crews of men were laying the tracks for the Kansas Pacific Railroad at this time. Meat was needed to feed them and Bill Cody was hired as a buffalo hunter. Great herds of the large beasts wandered the plains and in eighteen months Bill killed a total of 4,280, winning his famous nickname "Buffalo Bill." He did all his hunting on a horse named Brigham and used a rifle he dubbed "Lucretia Borgia."

In 1869 Buffalo Bill carried a number of army dispatches

through dangerous country in record time and was appointed chief of scouts for the Fifth Cavalry. The army couldn't have made a better choice and his work was greatly appreciated. In praising the scout, General Eugene A. Carr, his commanding officer, said, "Cody's eyesight is better than a good field glass. He is a perfect judge of distance and lay of the country."

During an exciting battle near War Bonnet Creek in 1876, Buffalo Bill was challenged to a duel by a Cheyenne Chief, Yellow Hand. All fighting stopped as the two rode against each other. On the second exchange of shots both Yellow Hand and his horse lay dead. Buffalo Bill and his horse were unhurt.

After acting in several Western plays, Buffalo Bill organized his own "Wild West Show" in 1883. With a huge cast of real cowboys and Indians, Cody's show told the thrilling story of the old West. There were Indian war dances, buffalo hunts, Pony Express riders, a real stagecoach, bareback riding and sharpshooting. But the great thrill of the performance was the entrance of Buffalo Bill astride his beautiful white horse.

The show was a spectacular success for years and played in hundreds of American and European cities.

Buffalo Bill Cody died in Denver, Colorado, on January 10, 1917. He is buried on Lookout Mountain, near Denver, in a tomb blasted from solid rock.

Our Greatest
Humorous Writer

ANYONE WHO has read Mark Twain's wonderfully entertaining story, *The Adventures of Tom Sawyer*, knows a great deal more about the author's boyhood than can be told here. The reason is that Mark Twain was really writing about himself and his friends when he wrote about Tom Sawyer. Nearly everything that happens to Tom in the book once happened to his creator.

Besides *Tom Sawyer*, Twain wrote many other great books, most of them based on his own experiences. His style of writing was completely original. Americans had never read anything to compare with his tales. They had never laughed quite so hard, and they kept asking for more and more.

When Mark Twain was a boy on the Mississippi it never occurred to him that he would become a writer. As far back as he

112

could remember he had dreamed of piloting one of the big Mississippi river boats. When that dream came true and he really was a pilot, Twain felt that he had achieved everything he wanted in this world. If it hadn't been for the Civil War, perhaps he would have kept right on being a pilot without ever writing any books. What a loss that would have been to the world!

Mark Twain was born in the little town of Florida, Missouri, on November 30, 1835. At that time, however, he wasn't called Mark Twain. His name was Samuel Langhorne Clemens, and he was the son of John and Jane Clemens. Mark Twain was a pen name he took many years later.

When little Sam was four, the Clemens family moved to Hannibal, Missouri, on the Mississippi River. Here the boy had many of the adventures he later wrote about. One of Sam's best friends was Tom Blankenship whom you know as "Huckleberry Finn."

Sam was sent to school when he was five. He got into trouble almost immediately. After several warnings, the teacher sent him out to get a switch with which she could punish him. Sam was back in five minutes, but instead of the stick the teacher expected, he brought her a curly wood shaving. That was Sam's idea of the right kind of switch!

Later he had a teacher named Cross. One day in school Sam made up this verse:

Cross by name and Cross by nature
Cross jumped over an Irish potato.

At noon one of the other boys copied the verse on the blackboard. When the teacher saw it he really was cross. The boy who copied the verse got a whipping but he didn't tell who had made it up and Sam got off scot free.

Sam never liked school. He won a medal for excellence in spelling every year, but not even the thrill of receiving this made up for the long days indoors. After much begging, he was allowed to leave school when he was twelve. Sam learned the printing trade and worked at this until he was twenty-one.

Then one fine day Sam stepped aboard a southbound Mississippi river boat. He intended to go to South America to make his fortune. But as the boat came alive beneath his feet, the old urge to become a pilot returned. Before the day was up, he had persuaded the gruff but kind-hearted pilot to take him on as a "cub-pilot."

Do you know what it meant to be a pilot on the Mississippi in those days? It meant knowing every inch of the way for twelve hundred miles—knowing every twist of the river, every turn, every island, every sandbar, every stump, every snag, every point, every bluff, every sounding. And knowing them in the pitchy black of night as perfectly as in the bright light of day.

Learning all this was hard, even for a smart young man like Sam, but by the end of a year he was as good a pilot as any on the river. For four years he sailed up and down the broad Mississippi, happier than he had ever been, never dreaming that one day he would write about all he saw in a book called *Life on the Mississippi*. But then the Civil War broke out. Passenger boats had to be taken off the river and Sam returned to Hannibal.

Shortly afterward Sam and his brother, Orion, went west to Nevada. The two men rode all the way—seventeen hundred miles— in a coach drawn by sixteen horses.

Everyone in Nevada had "gold fever." Sam caught it, too, but he soon gave up mining to become a reporter on a Nevada newspaper. After awhile he started signing his articles, but instead of using his own name he signed "Mark Twain."

"Mark Twain" was a call the writer had often heard on the Mississippi. Every river boat had a leadsman to keep the pilot informed of the water's depth. As he took each sounding the leadsman called out the number of fathoms. "Mark four," he'd call, or "Mark three." Or, when the water was two fathoms deep, "Mark twain."

Mark Twain made his first ocean voyage in 1866 when he was sent to Hawaii by the *Sacramento Union*. When he came back to America he gave a lecture about the trip. Although he had always been popular as a storyteller among his friends, he was amazed to see how many hundreds of people were more than glad to pay to hear him talk. After that he made many, many lectures.

The first of the great humorist's books appeared in May, 1867. It was called *The Celebrated Jumping Frog of Calaveras County and Other Sketches*. Mark Twain's other books include *The Innocents Abroad, Roughing It, The Prince and the Pauper*, and, of course, *The Adventures of Tom Sawyer* and *The Adventures of Huckleberry Finn*.

In 1870 the author married Olivia Langdon, a charming and intelligent woman. Within a few years he was able to give her a beautiful home in Hartford, Connecticut. Here they lived happily for seventeen years with their three daughters.

Mark Twain was a generous and soft-hearted man. He was nearly always ready to take a chance when someone asked him to back some scheme or invention. He lost a great deal of money this way, but he was sure he had a winner at last when he was approached by the inventor of a type-setting machine. It *was* a wonderful machine but it wasn't practical. In the end it cost Twain every cent he had and left him deeply in debt.

To get money to pay off these debts, the humorist made a lecture tour that took him around the world. He also wrote a book about the trip. His hard work and honesty won him more friends than ever.

Mark Twain liked white suits and looked especially well in

them, with his great shock of longish white hair. He smoked many cigars and loved to play billiards. The billiard room in his home was always red.

Following the death of his wife in 1903, Mark Twain lived for a time in New York, then in Redding, Connecticut. There, on April 21, 1910, a week after returning from a trip to Bermuda, America's favorite humorist died, bringing to a close a full and eventful life.

Elias Howe

Inventor of the Sewing Machine

ELIAS HOWE, inventor of the sewing machine, started life with two strikes against him. His parents were desperately poor. His health was frail and a crippled leg made him lame. Doggedly he refused to recognize these handicaps. He surmounted them and many other barriers to perfect the invention which has proved a boon to all mankind.

Howe was a simple, kindly man with a flair for mechanics. One day he overheard a chance remark that the world had great need of a mechanical device for sewing. The idea haunted him; he could not forget it. Finally he decided to attempt what then seemed impossible. The task was to demand years of worry, work, skimping and sorrow.

Because Howe was as poor as his parents had been, he naturally hoped to profit by his invention, but he was also inspired

117

by something else: the remembrance of his mother sewing by candlelight in a cold, dreary room long after the others had gone to bed; the sight of his wife's tired, workworn fingers taking stitch after stitch in the never-ending task of making, and making over, her family's clothing. For, strange as it now seems, less than a hundred years ago, every bit of clothing worn by every man, woman and child everywhere was made by hand.

Elias Howe, son of Elias Howe, was born at Spencer, Worcester County, Massachusetts, on July 9, 1819. His ancestors had settled in that state as early as 1640. Elias's father was a farmer and owner of a small grist- and saw-mill.

During the winter months Elias attended school, but the rest of the year he was kept busy at home. From the time he was six years old, he had regular chores, though his health was too frail to allow him to do any heavy work. He was especially good at helping around the mill since he had a natural liking for tools and machinery.

When twelve years old, Elias was hired out to a neighboring farmer, but farm work proved too much for the boy and he had to give it up after a year.

Realizing that his parents were too poor to keep him at home, Elias was constantly looking for other work. "Do you know of a job I could do?" he would ask every caller at the mill.

Eventually, at a friend's suggestion, he obtained a position in Lowell, working for a cotton machinery manufacturer. When the panic of 1837 caused the factory to shut down, Elias moved to Cambridge, then to Boston, where he went to work for a man named Ari Davis. Mr. Davis supplied Harvard professors with scientific apparatus.

Young Howe soon became a skilled and clever mechanic. He also met many of the inventors who came to Mr. Davis with models or new ideas.

While looking at a model one day, Mr. Davis remarked to its

maker, "What the world really needs is a machine to take the place of hand sewing. Why don't you concentrate on that?"

Working near by, Elias overheard Davis's comment. A sewing machine? What a wonderful idea! The more he thought of it, the more interested he became. Finally, he knew he would never rest until he, himself, had invented such a machine.

Howe started experimenting during the evening hours, at first trying to imitate the action of his wife's swift needle. Every attempt failed. Then one night he suddenly realized that he had been worrying more about the *method* than about the *result*. Perhaps a stitch could be made another way, quite different from the motion of the human hand.

This was the turning point toward success. Discarding all his former ideas, Howe started working with a needle that had its eye near the point instead of the head. Within a matter of days, he had thought of how a shuttle might be used along with the needle to make a lockstitch.

How pleased and excited he was! But pleasure gave way to discouragement. He would never be able to build the intricate machine needed to make such a stitch unless he could give up his job and work on nothing else.

Just as everything seemed hopeless, an old friend, George Fisher, came to the rescue. He lent Howe five hundred dollars to buy materials and opened his home to the man and his family.

Throughout the winter of 1844-45 Howe labored constantly. By April he had completed a machine that would sew smoothly and evenly.

A few months later he asked several tailors to test it. None was interested. Howe then went to the owner of a large dressmaking shop and challenged him to enter his five fastest hand sewers in a race against the machine. The machine, Howe said, would beat all five. And so it did. Even the fastest of the seamstresses could do only thirty-five stitches a minute while the machine could do two hundred and fifty.

In spite of this successful exhibition, the public remained uninterested. Howe was discouraged but realized he must get his machine patented. Again Fisher came to his aid with money for the trip to Washington and for patent fees. The patent was granted September 10, 1846.

By borrowing more money and sending his brother to London to demonstrate the machine, Howe finally made his first sale. An English manufacturer bought both machine and British rights for only $1,250.

Later Howe himself went to London but his association with the manufacturer turned out badly. The unfortunate inventor was stranded, penniless. To obtain passage back to America he was forced to pawn his first machine. En route he earned his meals by cooking for the steerage passengers.

Soon after his return to America his loyal wife died. Howe was heartsick, and to add to his dejection, he discovered that imitations of his sewing machine were being marketed in many American cities.

Determined to get what was lawfully his, he took his case to court. One of the longest fights in American patent law followed. It lasted from 1849 to 1854, but it was finally decided that Howe's patent was basic and he was entitled to a royalty on every machine that infringed his patent. In the 1860's these royalties often reached four thousand dollars a week!

In 1867 he won the gold medal at the Paris exhibition with the perfected Howe machine. Later that year, on October third, he died at his home in Brooklyn, New York, when only forty-eight years old.

Alexander Hamilton

Giant of Public Finance

ALEXANDER HAMILTON had one of the most brilliant minds of anyone who has ever called America his home. During the first hectic years following the adoption of our Constitution, he did as much or more to organize the federal government into a smoothly functioning unit than any other one person. As the country's first Secretary of the Treasury, he was faced with problems so great that no one less than a genius could have solved them.

Hamilton was a man who made many political enemies during his lifetime. He resented criticism. He was vain and jealous. Yet he accomplished so much, his many faults are all but overlooked. Without this wizard of finance and organization, the United States might have been many more years becoming the world power it is today.

He was born January 11, 1757, on a large plantation in the West Indies. Because his parents were then very wealthy, people often say, "Alexander Hamilton was born with a gold spoon in his mouth." But when he was only a boy of eleven, his father lost all his money. His mother died shortly before, so Alexander went to live with relatives.

However, even as a youngster he wanted to be independent and soon took a job as clerk in the store of a man named Nicholas Crugar. Here he did a man's work, but did it so well he was put in complete charge when Crugar took a trip to America.

Working every day, he had no chance to go to school, but he read a great deal and received a little instruction from a local minister. He also liked to write and soon developed a fine descriptive style.

Then came one of the most exciting experiences of his life. A hurricane swept through the West Indies. Crops were destroyed; trees were uprooted; houses were blown down. Lightning and thunder crashed through the sky and in the midst of all this terror, Alexander rode alone from the store to Mr. Crugar's plantation, carrying an important message.

Afterward he wrote a description of his ride. A newspaper published the article and it attracted such interest and praise that his friends were inspired to raise a fund to help him go to America to school.

For Alexander this was like having a dream come true! In 1773 he entered King's College (now Columbia University) in New York City, and continued his studies until 1775.

The Colonial cause aroused his immediate sympathy and while still in school he began speaking and writing in its behalf. Though he was only seventeen years old, his arguments were so sound and so well presented he made a great impression.

By the time war actually broke out, Hamilton had organized his own corps of volunteers. The uniforms of the group were green and brown. Their motto was "Freedom or death" and they called themselves the "Hearts of Oak."

Later this group became part of the regular New York militia. They were so brave in battle and such good soldiers, Washington became interested in their leader, and made Hamilton his aide-de-camp, or secretary.

During the next four years, no one was closer to the commander in chief. Washington discussed his many problems with Hamilton and entrusted him with important military missions. Hamilton wrote many of the general's letters and messages and his strong writing style helped put across Washington's ideas.

Soon people were calling him the "Little Lion," for while Hamilton had become mighty in his influence, he was a small man physically—below medium height and built proportionately.

At times the "Little Lion" showed a sulky side to his nature. For example, one day he was asked to report immediately to General Washington, but he stopped on the way to chat with General Lafayette. Washington reprimanded him for keeping him waiting, and Hamilton stubbornly refused to continue as the general's secretary.

A few months later his request for a field command was granted. At the Battle of Yorktown he proved his courage by being the first to spring over a high wall into the enemy fort as he led his troops against the British.

Shortly before this battle, Hamilton had been married to Elizabeth Schuyler, the charming and witty daughter of General Philip J. Schuyler. Many of Hamilton's letters to his wife have been preserved and they reflect the deep feeling he always held toward her and their eight children. She was equally devoted and at the time of her death, fifty years after his, she was still wearing in a little bag attached to a necklace a tender poem he had written her seventy-five years before.

Following the war, Hamilton studied law, but before beginning his practice, he served for a short time as a delegate to the Continental Congress.

As a lawyer Hamilton had few equals. However, he was more concerned with the country's lack of unity than with his own practice. Recognizing the importance of a strong central government, he worked unceasingly to turn public opinion in that direction.

When the Constitutional Convention met in 1787, Hamilton was one of three New York delegates. He proposed an aristocratic republic, including a president and senators chosen for life, and state governors appointed by the federal authorities. This plan was rejected by the Convention and Hamilton took no further part in the Convention work, except to engage in the final debates.

Although Hamilton was not entirely satisfied with the document, he signed it, and on his return to New York fought tooth and nail for its acceptance. The opposition was strong, but his eloquence was stronger and the state convention finally voted for ratification.

In 1789 Hamilton was made Secretary of the Treasury and the work he accomplished during the next six years would have done him credit had it taken a lifetime. Among other things, he induced Congress to pay the Revolutionary debts of the Continental Congress at par, and to assume the Revolutionary debts of the States. He worked out a complete system of national taxation. He was instrumental in the establishment of the first Bank of the United States.

Among his admirers, Hamilton became known as "the nation builder." But he also had powerful opponents. Many patriotic Americans, including Thomas Jefferson, were against such a strong federal government. The two groups organized into political parties, known as "Federalists," and "Anti-Federalists" or "Republicans."

In 1793 the controversy between Jefferson and Hamilton became so heated, Jefferson resigned as Secretary of State. Two years later, Hamilton also gave up his Cabinet post. Declining an opportunity to become Chief Justice of the U.S. Supreme Court, he returned to law practice.

Hamilton's influence, however, continued to be felt. Washington frequently consulted with him and it is said that during John Adams's term as president, the Cabinet was completely under his thumb.

Bitterest of all Hamilton's political enemies was Aaron Burr, a New York lawyer, who lost three important elective positions, including the presidency, largely through Hamilton's influence. Burr interpreted his actions as a personal insult and challenged him to a duel with pistols.

The two men met on the morning of July 11, 1804. Hamilton fired his pistol into the air, but Burr shot to kill and Hamilton was mortally wounded. He died the following day and is buried beside his wife in old Trinity Churchyard in the heart of New York's financial district. There office workers and tourists daily look down on the simple stone marking the last resting place of this man who played so important a role in the building of our great nation.

Francis Scott Key

Composer of
Our National Anthem

"GIVE ME the making of the songs of a nation, and I care not who makes its laws."

Strangely enough, Francis Scott Key, author of *The Star Spangled Banner*, our national anthem, was both a song maker and a lawmaker. Son of John Ross Key, he was born August 1, 1779, on the family estate in Frederick County, Maryland.

The Keys were wealthy, cultured people and Francis was given every advantage, including an education in law at St. John's College, Annapolis. Quick to learn and intelligent, the youth sincerely liked to study, but enjoyed outside amusements, too. He took part in social activities, was an ardent sportsman and always kept himself in trim. Throughout his life, he was slim and straight as an arrow.

Following graduation from St. John's, young Key began his

law practice in the village of Frederick, but soon moved to
Washington, D.C. He was district attorney there under Presidents Jackson and Van Buren.

While a student, Key had fallen in love with pretty Mary
Taylor Lloyd of Annapolis. She had many suitors but none more
persistent than Key who poured out his heart in tender love
poems. In 1802 they were married. During their long happy life
together they became the parents of six sons and five daughters.

In 1812 war broke out between Great Britain and the United
States. Two years later the British invaded and burned Wash-
ington, then retreated to their ships in the Patuxent River off
Chesapeake Bay. Among their prisoners was Dr. William
Beanes, a prominent physician.

As an attorney, Key was asked to try to obtain the doctor's
release. Key agreed and, accompanied by Colonel J. S. Skinner,
a government agent, he set out to call on the British Admiral.

Today the trip from Washington to the mouth of the Patuxent can be made in a matter of hours. In 1814 it took about three
days by stagecoach and sailboat.

Key found the enemy admiral reluctant to release Beanes,
but he finally relented. In the meantime, however, the British
had completed plans for an attack on Baltimore. To assure se-
crecy, Key and Skinner had to be held until the engagement
was over.

On September 13 the attack began. While British troops
marched on the city, the ships in the bay began bombardment
of near-by Fort McHenry, where a relative of Key was second
in command.

All day long the British rained shells on the little fort, while
Key and his companions watched from the deck of the *Min-
den*. At sunset the Stars and Stripes still flew above the fort, but
the British with longer range guns had the advantage. Could
the Americans hold out through a night of such relentless

pounding?

Eventually Skinner went below to try to sleep, but Key was too worried to rest. Throughout the night he paced the deck, tense with anxiety, fearful of what the morning might reveal.

Dawn came at last, but a pall of smoke obscured the fort. Not until the sun broke through could Key make out the battle-scarred flag of the United States. One of its fifteen stars had been torn out by a shell, but no banner ever looked more beautiful. The attack had failed! Key was overjoyed.

Some say the first draft of *The Star Spangled Banner* was hastily scribbled on an envelope even as he stood there watching. Others report he wrote it while going ashore that morning. In any event the verses were completed within twenty-four hours, eloquently expressing his love of God and country.

Adapted to the tune of "Anacreon in Heaven," the song immediately gained nationwide popularity and continued to be sung year after year.

Francis Scott Key died suddenly at the height of his career, on January 11, 1843, while visiting a daughter in Baltimore. He is buried in Frederick where the American flag flies over his grave both day and night. Nowhere else is this officially allowed.

On March 3, 1931, by act of Congress, *The Star Spangled Banner* was declared the national anthem of the United States. The act came as a surprise to millions for practically all foreign nations and many Americans had long accepted it as our national song.

'The flag which inspired his immortal poem is in the National Museum at Washington, D.C.

Inventor of the Telegraph

ARE YOU surprised when you pick up a newspaper and read about some happening that has taken place in Europe or Asia within the last twenty-four hours? Of course you aren't, but before the invention of the telegraph, it took more than twenty-four hours for news to be carried just from Boston to New York. The telegraph shared honors with the steamboat in bringing the world closer together.

Samuel Finley Breese Morse, inventor of the telegraph, was born in Charlestown, Massachusetts, on April 27, 1791, the eldest son of the Rev. Jedidiah Morse, preacher, author and educator.

Finley, as his family called him, was given a fine education. He was sent to grammar school in Andover, Massachusetts, then to Phillips Academy at Exeter. From Phillips he went to Yale

129

and while there often wrote home about his interest in electricity. He made it a point to learn all he could about this powerful natural force, but for years thought of it only as a hobby. He wanted to make painting his career.

While in school, young Morse made many friends. He was courteous and studious and had a pleasant personality and good humor that won him a warm welcome everywhere.

At Yale his artistic ability was discovered and it wasn't long before he was spending all his extra time painting miniature portraits of his friends at five dollars each.

In 1811, a year after his graduation, Morse was sent to England to study art. There he soon showed that he had more than ordinary talent. His paintings were displayed in leading galleries and won a number of important prizes. He was especially successful as a painter of historical subjects and it was in this field that he planned to specialize.

Unfortunately, on his return to the United States, he found his countrymen more willing to praise his historical paintings than they were to buy them. However, when he became a traveling portrait painter, he had as many orders as he could fill. In South Carolina his miniatures were so popular that in one week he received orders for one hundred and fifty at sixty dollars each.

About this time, Morse married and a few years later settled in New York City. His career as a painter advanced steadily, and in 1826 he founded the National Academy of Design.

Following the successive deaths of his wife, father and mother, Morse went to Europe. On the return voyage in 1832, the idea of the telegraph was born.

One day while discussing electrical experiments with several fellow passengers, Morse remarked that he could see no reason why messages couldn't be sent by electricity. This was an entirely new idea, and from then on, Morse thought of little else.

By the time he reached New York he had made many sketches of the instrument he proposed to build to test his theory.

At first, Morse spent only spare time on his experiments. Art was still his chief interest, but when he was refused a commission to paint one of the rotunda panels in the national Capitol, he became discouraged and gave his full time to the telegraph.

He was very poor and had to live and work in a single room, using a discarded clock and other worthless pieces to make the parts he needed for his experiments.

Problem after problem had to be solved, but in January, 1838, the instrument was at last perfected. Morse gave several demonstrations and then applied to Congress for $30,000 to build a trial telegraph line between Baltimore and Washington.

His request was ridiculed. Hurt and bewildered, Morse raised enough money to go to Europe to ask for help there. Again he got nowhere. In 1843 he renewed his petition to Congress. The appropriation finally passed the House by a six-vote margin. It was sent to the Senate but on the last day of the session was still buried beneath a stack of other bills. All day long Morse remained in the spectators' gallery. The session continued into the evening. At ten o'clock he gave up hope and went back to his inn.

Early the next morning Morse had a caller. It was Annie Ellsworth, daughter of the commissioner of patents, and the news she brought couldn't have been better. The Senate had passed the Morse Bill at midnight, just as the session adjourned! Morse was so elated he promised Annie she could supply the first message transmitted over the trial line.

The inventor kept his promise, too. In May 24, 1844, when the big moment came, it was Annie who chose the words of that famous first message, flashed to Baltimore from the United States Supreme Court in Washington: "What God hath wrought!" She had taken the words from the Bible.

Morse offered the Government rights to his patent, but Congress refused, believing the telegraph could never be made to pay for itself. A private company was formed and within a few years thousands of miles of lines were in operation.

Honors of all kinds were showered on the inventor, including an honorary degree from Yale, decorations from the rulers of many foreign lands and large gifts of money.

Looking ahead to a transatlantic cable, Morse experimented with a submarine telegraph line in New York harbor. He lived to see the Atlantic project successfully carried out in 1866.

Morse divided his last years between his two beautiful homes, one in New York and the other on the Hudson River, living comfortably and well as he richly deserved.

S.F.B. Morse died in New York on April 2, 1872, at the age of eighty-one years, an occasion for national mourning.

Booker T. Washington

American Educator

BORN IN slavery, Booker T. Washington gave his life to helping his people gain economic independence through practical education. With only a tumble-down shanty in which to begin, he established Tuskegee Normal and Industrial Institute and built it into one of America's great educational institutions. Tuskegee has become a lasting monument to the energy, resourcefulness and deep sincerity of this remarkable man.

Booker Taliaferro Washington was born in Franklin County, Virginia, the son of a Negro slave. The year of his birth was either 1858 or 1859. He never knew the exact date nor the name of his father. Named Booker Taliaferro by his mother, he added the "Washington" himself when he started school.

Booker's mother was a plantation cook. She and her three children lived in a one-room cabin with a dirt floor and no glass

133

in the windows. At one end of the cabin was the fireplace and in the center of the floor was a potato hole for storing sweet potatoes. Booker and his brother and sister slept on a heap of old rags. They ate whenever their mother found time to give them a bit of corn bread or pork. On Sunday they received a special treat sent down by their master—two tablespoonfuls of molasses apiece!

Then came the great day in 1865 when all the slaves were called to the plantation house and Lincoln's Emancipation Proclamation was read. They were free!

Booker's mother immediately set off on foot with the children to join her husband, a run-away slave then across the mountains in Malden, West Virginia. Unhappily, when they reached their new home they found it was as poor a place as the one they had left, and the surroundings were far less wholesome. In addition, the stepfather insisted that the two little boys work in a near-by salt furnace.

At Malden, however, Booker received his first taste of learning. After teaching himself the alphabet, he attended school for a short time and learned to read. Now determined to get a real education, he set out for Hampton Normal and Agricultural Institute in Virginia when he was fourteen. Hampton was five hundred miles away and by the time he reached Richmond his little hoard of nickels and quarters was gone. To earn enough to continue his journey, he went to work on the docks, sleeping under a wooden sidewalk at night.

Finally reaching Hampton, he earned his board by serving as janitor. His tuition was paid by a generous Yankee.

To Booker, Hampton was like another world. For the first time he slept between sheets, used a toothbrush and learned to bathe regularly. Tablecloths and napkins were something new to him, too. Everything, including the classwork, was exciting and wonderful. Most of all, however, Booker appreciated the friendship of the Institute's president, wise and good General Samuel C. Armstrong.

Following his graduation, young Washington spent two years teaching in Malden, then took advanced work in Washington, D.C. In 1879 he became an instructor at Hampton.

Two years later, on the recommendation of General Armstrong, Washington was named head of a new school for Negroes to be started in Tuskegee, Alabama. Thrilled with this opportunity, Washington traveled joyfully south.

In Tuskegee, to his dismay, he found that while the legislature had appropriated two thousand dollars annually for salaries, no provision had been made for buildings. However, he soon arranged to use a dilapidated church and shanty.

Next he set out to round up students and in doing so realized more fully than ever the importance of his work. It was obvious in nearly every home he visited that, while his people appreciated their freedom, they still had to be taught to use it properly.

On July 4, 1881, Tuskegee Normal and Industrial Institute held classes for the first time. Thirty students attended and within six weeks there were twenty more. Soon the school was moved to an old plantation. Here the buildings were dilapidated, too, but the students were put to work making them usable. They were then asked to spend several hours daily helping raise crops. A number objected but Washington insisted. He knew that there were two lessons all his students must learn: the importance of cleanliness and the dignity of labor.

As funds for new buildings were obtained, all actual building was done by the students under supervision. Thus, they received practical instruction in carpentry, masonry and other trades. The girls, too, devoted their time in sewing and cooking classes to the production of things that could be put to practical use.

With the passing years, Washington spent more and more time traveling through the country talking about Tuskegee and raising money to further the good work of the school. The whole United States responded warmly and generously to his appeals. Everywhere he went his fine personality and great good humor won him friends. His outstanding accomplishments as an educator were given recognition in many ways, including a visit by President William McKinley and his Cabinet to the Tuskegee Institute. Honorary degrees were conferred upon Booker T. Washington by Harvard University and Dartmouth College.

Washington's many books include *Future of the American Negro* and his autobiography, *Up From Slavery*.

Booker T. Washington died on November 14, 1915, admired and respected throughout the world.

Daniel Boone

Pioneer Scout and Patriot

WHEN PEOPLE talk about Daniel Boone, they think of a tall, lean, muscular man wearing a buckskin jacket and coonskin cap and carrying a long, old-fashioned gun. Often they dismiss the tales told of this early pathfinder as being imaginary stories. Nothing could be farther from the truth, for Daniel Boone lived a dangerous, exciting life most of his eighty-six years.

This loyal patriot's services to our country in its early days can never be measured in dollars and cents. His Wilderness Road opened up land to hundreds of thousands of settlers and paved the way to the winning of all the West. Yet a few years before his death he found himself without an acre of land he could call his own.

Daniel Boone was a lover of peace, although he spent many

137

years of his life fighting hostile Indians. He was a modest man, moderate in all things, but brave as a lion, and nearly as strong. He was true to his family and friends and treated everyone fairly.

Born in November, 1734, on a wilderness farm near Reading, Pennsylvania, Daniel was one of eleven children. His father, Squire Boone, had come to America from England.

Daniel loved the frontier life. He was a crack shot and an expert hunter and could move through the forest without making a sound. When it came to finding or breaking a trail, no one could equal him.

There were no schools near by, but Daniel managed to learn to read and write at home. He also acquired a little knowledge of arithmetic, and his father taught him the trades of blacksmith and wagoner.

When Daniel was about sixteen, the Boone family moved from Pennsylvania to North Carolina. The boy enjoyed the trek through new country and longed to see more of America. As a result, a few years later when General Braddock called for men to fight the French and Indians in western Pennsylvania, young Boone was among the first to volunteer.

His next long trip was into western Tennessee. Here he carved these words on a tree beside the stream now called Boone's Creek: "D. Boon killed a bar on this tree in the year 1760."

In 1769, Boone was hired by some land speculators to explore Kentucky, then completely wild and unsettled. Heading an expedition of six men, he arrived there safely and had been hunting and exploring for some time when Indians swooped down on the camp. All six white men were captured but were soon turned loose with a warning to return East immediately. The Indians gave them a little food but kept their horses, furs and supplies.

Boone was determined to get the horses back. Stealing into the Indian camp at night, he and one of his companions, named Stewart, managed to make away with four of the animals. The loss was quickly discovered, however, and the two men were captured.

Wise to the ways of the Indians, Boone told Stewart to pretend he liked being with them. By the end of seven days the white men seemed so friendly and happy, the Indians relaxed their guard. That night when Boone was sure their captors slept, he awakened Stewart and they made their escape.

The other four men soon returned home, but Boone and Stewart were joined by Boone's brother, Squire, and a friend who brought fresh horses and supplies.

One day Stewart disappeared. When no trace of him could be found, the frightened fourth man decided to go home. Later Squire made a trip back to North Carolina for supplies. While he was gone, Daniel remained completely alone, without any bread or salt. In a few months Squire returned and the two brothers continued their explorations. Finally in March, 1771, the two returned East together.

Two years later they decided to move to Kentucky with their families. A number of other families joined them, and at Cumberland Gap Indians attacked the party. Several of the pioneers were killed, Boone's eldest son, Jamie, among them. The caravan then decided to stop for a while.

During this period Boone was chosen by the Transylvania Company, dealers in land, to make a road through the wilderness from the Wautauga Settlements in Tennessee to the Kentucky River. He had thirty woodsmen to help him and together they cut, burned and fought their way through two hundred miles of virgin forest and undergrowth to build the now-famous Wilderness Road. When they had completed this gigantic task they set about building cabins and a stockade fort. Here it was that Boone brought his wife and family to live. Mrs. Boone and their daughters were the first white women to stand on the banks of the Kentucky River.

Life was dangerous even for the children. One summer day Indians captured one of Boone's daughters and two little playmates. Boone quickly trailed them and rescued the girls.

While on an expedition to the Blue Licks for salt, Boone was taken prisoner by a band of Shawnee Indians. For four months he was in their hands. However, he was well treated because again he pretended to be happy and to like the Indians' way of living. He was such a good actor the Shawnees became very fond of him and adopted him into the tribe. Boone continued his pretense. He had all his hair pulled out except a scalp lock, and he painted his face with bright yellow and other colors. By this time the red men even allowed him to go hunting, but kept careful track of his ammunition.

Then one day he learned that the Shawnees were planning an attack on Boonesboro. Securing permission to go hunting alone, he immediately started on foot for the fort, one hundred sixty miles away, with hardship and danger every step of the way. Day and night Boone pushed on, without food, without sleep, with only one thought in mind—to warn his family and friends as quickly as possible so they might prepare special defenses. In less than five days he reached his goal!

About six weeks later the attack came. Although outnumbered six to one, Boone and his men won the battle and drove off the Indians.

A few years after Kentucky was admitted to the Union, Boone learned that all the land he had staked and claimed was not legally his because he had neglected to secure clear titles for the property.

In disgust, he moved to Missouri where he was given land by the Spanish authorities. He made the mistake of settling near, but not on this property, and again lost his holdings when the United States gained possession of this region. A year later the land was returned to him by an act of Congress.

Daniel Boone lived to be eighty-six years old and enjoyed hunting and fishing until almost the time of his death. He died in September, 1820, and was buried in Missouri. Later his body and that of his wife were removed to Frankfort, Kentucky, where a monument was erected to his memory.

Andrew Jackson

"Old Hickory"

ANDREW JACKSON was a man of the people—honest, sincere, courageous and strong-willed—loved by his friends and hated by his enemies.

As a general in the War of 1812, he proved a brilliant leader and won a spectacular victory at New Orleans, the anniversary of which is still celebrated in Louisiana.

Andrew Jackson was born on March 15, 1767, in the Waxhaw Settlement on the border between North and South Carolina, just a few days after the death of his father for whom he was named. The Jacksons, with their two older sons, Robert and Hugh, had come to America from Ireland shortly before. They were very poor but had found great happiness in their backwoods home.

Andrew grew into a sturdy, freckled-faced boy, quick-tempered and independent. With his brothers, he attended school

142

for two years but was not sorry when his teacher enlisted in the Continental Army and the school had to be closed. He had especially disliked spelling.

When only thirteen, Andrew, too, enlisted. Unhappily, however, he and his brothers were soon captured by the British.

At the prison camp, a British officer one day sharply ordered Andrew to black his boots. The boy's blood boiled. He was a prisoner of war, and the officer had no right to make this demand. Defying his captor, Andrew flatly refused.

Now it was the officer's turn to be furious. Shouting his rage, he swung at the boy with his sword, cutting him on the wrist and head. Andrew never lost the scars left by those wounds, nor the hatred of the British which they planted in him.

While in captivity, Hugh died of a wound, and soon after their release, both Andrew and Robert came down with smallpox. Robert failed to recover and soon afterward Mrs. Jackson died. At fifteen, Andrew was completely alone.

Without love or guidance, the youth lived aimlessly for several years. Finally at twenty, he began to study law, working hard and seriously. He was admitted to the bar and settled in the Western District of North Carolina, later Tennessee. Shrewd, capable and honest, the young lawyer made many friends and built up a thriving practice.

In 1791 he married Rachel Robards and took her to live in The Hermitage, his lovely, new, white-pillared home near Nashville. No couple could have been more devoted and Jackson never forgave the slanderous remarks some of his enemies made about Rachel.

When Tennessee was admitted to the Union, Jackson was elected to Congress. Two years later, in 1798, he was made judge of the Supreme Court of Tennessee and served for six years.

As commander in chief of the Tennessee militia, he and his

men volunteered at the outbreak of the War of 1812. In 1814 they achieved final victory over the hostile Creek Indians. Following the decisive battle, Jackson learned that a baby Indian boy had been left without father or mother. When the Creek squaws refused to care for him, Jackson took the tiny redskin home to The Hermitage where the child lived happily until his death from tuberculosis at seventeen.

Jackson was commissioned a major general in the regular army and given command of the Department of the South. His victory at New Orleans on January 8, 1815, marked him as the greatest general in the war.

Leading an army of six thousand men, he won a complete victory over more than twice that many British in one of the shortest battles on record. It took Jackson just half an hour to turn the enemy's bold advance into full retreat. More than two thousand British dead and wounded, including their general, were left on the battlefield, as against only a sprinkling of Americans.

Jackson was the nation's hero. He became governor of Florida when the territory was purchased from Spain, and later he was elected U.S. Senator. In 1824 he narrowly missed becoming president of the United States and in 1828 was elected to that office by a large majority.

The next eight years were stormy ones for Jackson. Certain groups felt he did not belong to the circle from which a president should be chosen, but the common people regarded him as the greatest leader of the times. American democracy achieved new strength during Jackson's time.

Believing firmly in a strong federal government, Jackson quickly crushed South Carolina's attempt to nullify a new tariff law. His patriotism, courage and inflexible will were clearly shown as he heatedly declared, "The Union must, and shall be preserved! Send for General Scott!" Fortunately military force did not have to be used, but it is easy to see how Jackson got his nickname, "Old Hickory."

When Jackson retired from office in 1836, he had a greater following than ever, and throughout the rest of his life friends and well-wishers flocked to see him at The Hermitage. He died there on June 8, 1845, and was buried in the garden beside his wife.

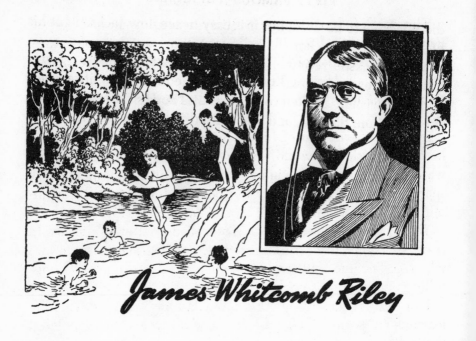

James Whitcomb Riley

The Hoosier Poet

ONE OF the favorite poets of all American school children is James Whitcomb Riley. His tender and humorous verse is easy to read and understand and nearly always tells the kind of story that boys and girls especially enjoy.

Riley is called "the Hoosier Poet" because he was a resident of Indiana and because he wrote many of his poems in the Hoosier dialect—a manner of speaking used by the country people of Indiana back in the 1860's and 1870's.

James Whitcomb Riley was born in Greenfield, Indiana, on October 7. Some say the year was 1853; others say 1848 or '49. The reason for this difference of opinion is that Riley never told his exact age when he grew old. To his friends and admirers he always seemed young.

The poet's father, Reuben A. Riley, was a farmer and lawyer. From his mother, little James inherited a great love of nature. He knew the names of all the wild flowers. He could recognize every bird call. He felt sure that there could be nothing quite so beautiful as an Indiana sunset, unless it was an Indiana sunrise.

Swimming was one of his favorite sports. As early as April, he and his friends would be down testing the warmth of the water in their favorite swimming hole. By June they spent every spare hour there. Years later the poet told about all the swimming fun in a poem called "The Old Swimmin' Hole."

Young Jim Riley wasn't much of a student, but he did like to read. Henry Wadsworth Longfellow was his favorite poet, and when he became a little older he usually had a book of Longfellow's poems in his pocket.

During his teens Riley got a job as a house painter. Then he learned to paint signs and for several years he wandered through Indiana painting signs for businessmen. Sometimes he worked in the city; sometimes in the country, where he painted advertising messages on fences and barns.

Later he became an actor in an old-time traveling "medicine show." A medicine show was usually put on by a person selling patent medicine. He hired entertainers to draw a crowd, then sold his product to the audience.

Traveling about this way, Riley learned a lot about Indiana. He discovered that people on Indiana farms and in the small towns spoke a dialect all their own. He found that they had their own ideas and customs. Whenever he had a few minutes to spare, he wrote poems about these people—some in pure English, others in the Indiana dialect.

A number of Riley's verses were printed in Indiana newspapers, but at first they didn't make much of an impression. Riley decided to prove that it was just because he wasn't famous that his poems weren't appreciated. He wrote a poem in a style typical of Edgar Allen Poe and talked a newspaper editor into printing it. The poem was signed "E.A.P." and the editor wrote a little article saying that the poem had been discovered in Richmond, Virginia, written on the flyleaf of a dictionary.

Neither Riley nor the editor apparently realized what the reaction would be. All over the country newspapers reprinted the poem. Some critics said they did not believe Poe had written it; others decided it was probably genuine. Finally the editor had to explain that it was all a joke. Many people became very angry with young Riley and he feared that he might have ruined all his chances to become recognized as a poet.

However, not long afterward the *Indianapolis Journal* asked Riley to become a regular contributor to the paper. At first he used a nom de plume, or pen name, signing himself "Benjamin F. Johnson of Boone," but later he used his own name.

Readers of the *Journal* liked his Hoosier dialect poems very much, and in 1883 he published his first book of verse. This was called *The Old Swimmin' Hole and 'Leven More Poems*. Gradually, people outside of Indiana came to know and enjoy Riley's poetry. For years the Hoosier poet had admired Longfellow. Now it was Longfellow's turn to praise Riley's poems. James Russell Lowell, another American poet, also expressed admiration for them.

As Riley's popularity spread he was asked to appear in various cities to read his own poems. Wherever he went there would be a big turnout because his programs were always entertaining. He had a great gift of mimicry and a fine speaking voice.

Riley never married, but he loved children and they always received a warm welcome when they visited him. Sometimes on his birthday they staged a parade past his home. In 1915 the governor of Indiana declared the poet's birthday a day of celebration, and Riley programs were held in all the schools.

By this time James Whitcomb Riley had become a very wealthy man, but nothing ever made him happier than the recognition by the people of the state he loved so well.

Besides "The Old Swimmin' Hole," some of Riley's most popular poems are "The Raggedy Man," "Little Orphant Annie," and "When the Frost Is on the Punkin."

James Whitcomb Riley died at his home in Indianapolis on July 22, 1916.

George M. Cohan

Yankee Doodle Dandy

ON JUNE 29, 1936, the United States Congress passed an act awarding a gold medal to a song writer for writing two great patriotic songs.

George M. Cohan was the song writer. "Over There," written during World War I, and "It's a Grand Old Flag," written in 1905, were the songs. The Congressional Medal was personally presented to Cohan by President Franklin D. Roosevelt.

The man who received this signal honor was not only a song writer. He was also a dancer, singer, actor, playwright, director and producer—the most versatile man in the American theater.

Cohan was part of the theater from the day he was born—July 4, 1878, in Providence, Rhode Island. His Irish parents, Helen F. and Jerry J. Cohan, and his sister Josie were all show people.

Following theatrical tradition, little Georgie slept in the drawer of his parents' trunk until it could no longer hold him. After that he played backstage while his parents performed. In 1886, when Georgie was eight, he had his name on a program for the first time. In a wild west show called "Daniel Boone," he rode a donkey in the street parade that preceded the show, played the violin in the orchestra and sold songbooks on the side.

A year or so later, billed as a trick violinist, he played a week in Boston. He was to be paid what the manager thought his act was worth. When he found six dollars in his pay envelope, Georgie gave up the violin.

At eleven he was doing a buck and wing dance. Two years later he was starring in *Peck's Bad Boy*, manfully taking, and giving, black eyes along with the applause. After every performance there was a crowd of boys at the stage door itching to make him prove he was as tough in real life as he was on the stage.

Peck's Bad Boy was the first show in which all four of the Cohans appeared. For the next fourteen years they refused to be separated and toured the country's vaudeville circuits billed as "The Four Cohans."

In 1896 when The Four made a terrific hit in Brooklyn, George made his first curtain speech, saying spontaneously with his best Irish grin, "Ladies and gentlemen, my mother thanks you, my father thanks you, my sister thanks you, and I thank you." The audience loved it and during his long career George must have repeated this little speech thousands of times.

The Four Cohans' first Broadway appearance was in 1902 in *The Governor's Son*, written by George, himself. The play was popular in many large cities, but Broadway was unenthusiastic.

George had been writing songs and vaudeville comedy sketches since he was fifteen. He sold his sketches on a royalty

basis and it was said that in the early 1900's he had an income
of nearly $50,000 from royalties alone. His first published song,
"Why Did Nellie Leave Home?" was written when he was fifteen.

During his teens, George seldom bothered to control his quick
Irish temper and was frequently in hot water with the theater
managers. He was also a very conceited young man. However,
as he grew older he became a modest person who rarely raised
his voice, though no one could ever "push him around."

When Cohan was twenty-six he joined forces with Sam H.
Harris, and they made a great success as partners for eighteen
years.

On Broadway Cohan set a pace no one could equal. His energy never seemed to give out. While starring in one of his own
plays, he would be rehearsing a second and perhaps writing a
third. His first Broadway hit was *Little Johnny Jones* in 1904.
He was both the writer and the star. From then on one success
followed fast upon another.

Cohan used to call himself "The Original Yankee Doodle
Boy—born on the Fourth of July" and there was nearly always
a patriotic note in his plays and songs.

The tune of "Over There," Cohan said, had "popped into his
head" one morning. By the time he reached his office he had the
refrain and first verse well in mind. The song proved very popular. Over a million and a half copies of this inspiring song were
sold.

Not the least of Cohan's accomplishments was his development from a vaudeville trouper to a dramatic actor capable of
handling expertly such roles as the country editor in Eugene
O'Neill's great play, *Ah, Wilderness*. But in spite of his success,
Cohan always insisted he was "just a song and dance man."

Cohan never liked working in motion pictures. The motion
picture people, in turn, never seemed to fully appreciate Cohan

until shortly before his death when *Yankee Doodle Dandy*, starring James Cagney as Cohan, was produced. Cohan was very ill by the time the picture was finished, but a special preview was held for him alone.

George M. Cohan died on November 5, 1942. His two daughters, his son and his wife were at his bedside. He is buried in New York.

John C. Fremont

The Pathfinder

A HUNDRED years ago, our west coast presented a far different picture than it does today. England and the United States were in joint possession of Oregon. California belonged to Mexico. Settlements were few and far between and there were many hostile Indians, especially in the north.

Many pioneers had already settled west of the Mississippi, but the Rockies and Sierras barred the path onward. A few had struggled north and west to Oregon, but the way was not clearly defined. They needed a leader to mark the route. John Charles Fremont became that leader. In a series of thrilling expeditions he made his way through the wildest kind of country to the coast, and all along the way he made careful observations so that he would be able to describe the country to others. He made maps. He kept records of latitude and longitude. He gathered specimens of plants and rocks. He studied the stars. All this information he compiled into reports that read like thrilling fiction and inspired thousands of Americans to pack their belongings into prairie schooners and make the long trip west. These reports were reprinted in many newspapers and Fremont was soon nicknamed "The Pathfinder."

Some grumblers objected, saying that Kit Carson was the real pathfinder. Certainly Carson was Fremont's good right hand and Fremont always gave him great credit, but Carson had neither the knowledge nor education to make the observations and write the reports that made Fremont's work so valuable in America's westward growth.

John Charles Fremont was born in Savannah, Georgia, on January 31, 1813. His father had come to America from his native France. His mother belonged to a distinguished Virginia family.

When John was five his father died. Mrs. Fremont and her three children returned to Virginia to live for a time, then moved to Charleston, South Carolina. There John studied Greek, Latin and mathematics. He also learned to tell direction and location by the stars, though he didn't realize then how useful this knowledge was going to be.

Young Fremont's first experience as an explorer came in 1838 as a second lieutenant in the topographical or map-making corps of the United States engineers. He was sent to Minnesota on an expedition with Jean Nicollet, an important French geographer.

When their field work was done, Fremont helped Nicollet make a map of the country they had covered. One of the men who saw and admired this map was Thomas Hart Benton, Senator from Missouri.

One evening Senator Benton took Fremont to his home for

dinner. It was love at first sight for the young explorer and the senator's sixteen-year-old daughter, Jessie, but both Jessie's parents disapproved of their romance because of her age. The couple finally decided to elope. Several ministers refused to marry them without the Senator's approval, but at last they were able to persuade a jolly Dutch priest to perform the ceremony for them.

Both were a little frightened of facing Jessie's father, but Senator Benton was a sensible man. Since it was now useless to object he gave his son-in-law a warm welcome.

Not long afterward Fremont asked the government for funds to make a trip of exploration into the unknown country beyond the Missouri river. There was some opposition, but with Benton's backing the request was eventually granted.

When Fremont left St. Louis in the spring of 1842, his goal was South Pass in the territory which is now Wyoming. Traveling up the Missouri River by boat, Fremont met just the man to make his expedition complete—Kit Carson. By the time they started overland, Kit had joined Fremont as guide.

Everything went well on the first expedition. There were hardships, of course, but by the end of October Fremont was back in Washington. There, with Jessie Fremont's help, he wrote a report that won highest praise from Congress.

Fremont received money for a second expedition almost immediately. This time Mrs. Fremont and their baby daughter went along as far as St. Louis and waited there for him to return.

About ten days after the explorer left St. Louis, a letter addressed to him arrived from the War Department. His wife was handling all his mail, so quickly tore it open. To her shocked surprise, the letter ordered Fremont to return to Washington at once to explain why he was taking a cannon with him on a scientific survey.

Mrs. Fremont's heart sank. Then quickly she decided, *he*

Fremont's Exploration Sent Caravans Westward

must not return! But a copy of the letter she held was undoubtedly on its way to Kaw's Landing where Fremont was spending several weeks fattening his horses. She must get a message to him before the letter arrived! Sending for a scout to carry the message, she dashed off a note. She gave no explanation but told her husband he must leave at once.

"Hurry!" she called after the scout as he left. "Hurry!" Two days later Fremont had the note. Though greatly puzzled by its contents he had complete faith in his wife's judgment and left immediately.

This time South Pass marked only the first lap of the journey. From there Fremont's party pushed on until one day in September they stood on the shore of the Great Salt Lake.

Curious about an island far out in the lake, Fremont, Carson and three others decided to investigate. They had brought along a collapsible india-rubber boat for just such excursions and were soon on their way.

Fremont was disappointed to find the island was nothing but barren rock so he named it Disappointment Island. However, there was a nice sandy beach on which to make camp and the men enjoyed a good night's sleep with no Indians to worry about. The island is now called Fremont Island.

By November they had reached the Oregon Territory. Here they restocked their supplies and started south into country completely unknown to everyone in the group. Soon they were in mountains deep with snow. The first two months of travel that followed were difficult but nothing compared to the third, spent in crossing west over the Sierras from what is now Nevada. Horses died of exposure and starvation. Supplies ran out and several of the animals had to be killed for food. But there was no complaining among these stout-hearted men. Inspired by their leader's outstanding courage they kept traveling on until at last, early in March, they reached Sutter's Fort on the Sacramento River.

They took only a few days to rest, however, and then set off again, south through the beautiful valley of the San Joaquin. Here the Sierras were easier to cross and by August eighth the expedition was safely back in St. Louis. Again Fremont's report was a masterpiece of thrilling detail. Ten thousand copies were printed, and more covered wagons than ever before started the westward trek.

Fremont's next expedition to California, in 1845-46, brought him into the war between the United States and Mexico and ended in his trial by court-martial. A dispute had arisen as to whether Fremont should take orders from General Kearny of the Army or Commodore Stockton of the Navy. Fremont felt his first loyalty was to Stockton because he had been acting on the commodore's orders long before Kearny arrived in California. As a result the general accused him of mutiny and ordered him East for trial.

Fremont was found guilty and sentenced to dismissal. President Polk remitted the sentence but, bitterly unhappy, the explorer resigned from the Army.

Shortly afterward he was hired to make a winter survey to the coast for a railroad company. Hard as the other trips had been, this was the worst of all. Eleven men were lost in the mountains during raging blizzards, and Fremont and the rest of his party were finally turned back by insurmountable barriers of ice and snow. They had just strength enough left to reach Kit Carson's home in Taos.

Jessie Fremont, meanwhile, had traveled to California by way of Panama with her daughter and after a rest Fremont joined them out there, taking a southerly route over the mountains.

Settling in the Golden State, Fremont was elected one of California's first United States senators. In 1856, he was the new

Republican party's first presidential candidate, and, though defeated, made a good showing.

The Civil War saw him back in uniform, but he resigned his commission in 1864. Fourteen years later he was appointed governor of the Arizona Territory and served for three years.

In 1890, while on a trip east from his beloved California, Fremont fell ill and died on July thirteenth. He is buried at Piermont, New York.

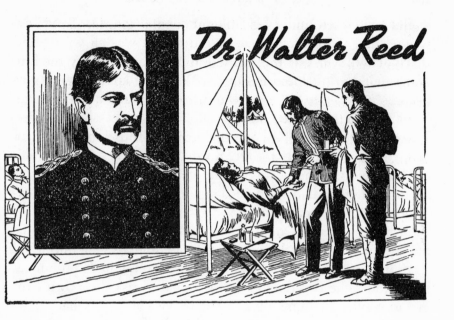

Dr. Walter Reed

Hero of
American Medicine

FIFTY YEARS ago yellow fever was one of Cuba's most deadly diseases. Occasionally an epidemic would strike our southern or eastern coast, too, and when it did as many as three out of every four of the sick might die. Whole families were often wiped out.

Doctors were helpless against the disease, because so little was known about it. No one knew its cause; worse still, no one knew how it was spread. Most scientists believed that yellow fever was contagious from person to person, like measles, but nobody had been able to prove this theory.

Then in June, 1900, Dr. Walter Reed, a friendly, mild-mannered major in the United States Army Medical Corps, was sent to Cuba to investigate the dread disease.

Within six months, through a series of ingenious experi-

161

ments conducted under his brilliant supervision, Dr. Reed had proved that the commonly accepted theory was all wrong and that yellow fever was transmitted in one way only—by the bite of a small, dark-colored mosquito. With this knowledge, it has become possible to wipe out the disease in Cuba and eliminate its danger to the United States.

Much hard work had been done during those six months of investigation—not only by Dr. Reed but by every medical officer on the board he headed. One of the doctors had given his life and another had become dangerously ill as a result of experimenting on themselves.

Ordinarily, certain animals can be used in such experiments, but it had soon been discovered that all animals generally used were immune to "yellow jack." Tests had to be made on human beings, and the two doctors had decided to risk their own lives in the service of humanity. Other brave volunteers had come forward, too, and Dr. Reed himself had offered to risk his life. He, however, was finally persuaded that his work was too important for him to do so.

The theory that the mosquito transmitted yellow fever was not original with Dr. Reed, but by proving the theory he made possible the control of the disease. The greatness of his work was recognized throughout the scientific world and he was given honorary degrees by both Harvard University and the University of Michigan.

Walter Reed was born in Belroi, Gloucester County, Virginia, on September 13, 1851, son of the Reverend Lemuel Sutter Reed, a Methodist circuit rider.

Probably the most exciting experience of Walter's boyhood was his "capture" by Union soldiers. Being southerners, the Reeds sided with the Confederacy in the Civil War, and on this occasion twelve-year-old Walter and his brother Christopher were hiding several horses from the invading Yankees.

After two days in a thick clump of trees the boys were finally discovered, and as the soldiers marched them down the road Walter and Christopher pictured themselves penned up for years in some prison camp. The Yankees, however, wanted only the horses. After several hours of suspense the boys were sent home.

In spite of frequent family moves young Walter attended school regularly. A conscientious student, he always stood high in his class and when only sixteen he was admitted to the University of Virginia.

At the end of a year young Reed decided to become a doctor. Studying harder than ever, he was able to pass the examination for a medical degree within twelve months. A few years later he received his second medical degree from Bellevue Hospital Medical College in New York, after which he was appointed Health Inspector by the newly created Metropolitan Board of Health.

The year 1874 was important for Dr. Reed: he decided to try for the Medical Corps of the United States Army, and he fell in love with good-humored, charming Emilie Lawrence. A year later he had his commission as assistant surgeon with the rank of first lieutenant and on April 25, 1876, he married Emilie.

For the next fourteen years the Reeds traveled from one army post to another, many of them on lonely frontiers, like Camp Lowell in Arizona and Fort Sidney in Nebraska. Two children were born to them, and their home was also shared by a young Indian girl, an orphan who had been brought to Dr. Reed for treatment of serious burns.

Dr. Reed gained invaluable experience in the various camps but as the years passed he longed for an opportunity to renew his studies. Great progress was being made in medicine, and he did not want to be left behind.

Naturally, therefore, he was overjoyed when, in 1890, he was ordered to Baltimore as attending physician and examiner of recruits. Some of America's foremost authorities in modern medicine were teaching at Johns Hopkins hospital in Baltimore and since Reed's new duties were fairly light he had plenty of time for study.

At Johns Hopkins he specialized in bacteriology, then a new branch of medicine. The laboratory director, Dr. William H. Welch, soon recognized Reed's outstanding ability as a bacteriologist. Reed, in turn, had found the field in which he belonged.

In 1893 it became possible for Dr. Reed to devote full time to teaching and research. Promoted to the rank of major, he was appointed professor of clinical and sanitary microscopy in the new Army Medical School, and curator of the Army Medical Museum.

During the Spanish-American War in 1898, United States citizens were shocked to learn that many more Americans were dying from tropical diseases than from enemy bullets. The war was over in a few months, but disease still ran rampant through the army camps, with malaria reported especially prevalent. An investigating board, headed by Dr. Reed, soon proved that many of the "malaria" cases were actually typhoid. The board also discovered how the disease was being spread in the camps and established methods of control.

Two years later Dr. Reed started his yellow fever investigation and when this work was completed returned to the Army Medical School.

On November 23, 1902, Dr. Walter Reed died in Washington, D.C. He is buried in Arlington National Cemetery. Not far distant is the greatest of many memorials to this great man—the Walter Reed Memorial Hospital.

Dolly Madison

Heroine in
the White House

WHEN JAMES MADISON became the fourth President of the United States, he brought with him into the White House a pretty wife whose grace and charm had already endeared her to the American people. For eight years, as first lady of the land, this former little Quaker girl was the toast of Washington society. Her warm humanity and ready tongue constantly won her new friends and admirers, and many thought that her husband's second election owed much to her popularity. To add to all this, seemingly enough glory for any American woman, she acted quickly and courageously in a crisis to save a national treasure for posterity.

"Dolly" Madison, born Dorothea Payne, was one of nine children of John and Mary Payne, Quakers. They were residents of Virginia, although Dolly was born in Guilford County, North Carolina, where the Paynes were temporarily making

165

their home in the year of 1768. It is said that she inherited her beauty from the Winstons and her ready tongue from the Irish Coles, both of whom were on her mother's side of the family.

Soon the family moved to "Scotchtown," which at one time had been Patrick Henry's Virginia estate. "Scotchtown" was a huge house, as you can see from the fact that it had a third-floor room one hundred feet long.

In the big house, the little Quaker girl sat with her mother in the "blue room" and learned to sew. She also watched the cooking being done in the great kitchen fireplace, with the use of spits and iron kettles.

Outdoors, Dolly could see all manner of interesting things taking place, for in those days a rural family was largely self-sufficient. There was carpentering, the making of cloth by spinning and weaving, preparation of meat and other food for storing and preserving, candle-making and many other activities to fascinate a growing child.

There too, Dolly must have learned the gracious ways that later made her famous, for good manners and hospitality were made points of great importance.

Dolly went to school long enough to learn to read and write and do a little figuring. Since girls were destined only to keep house and care for their husbands and children when they grew up, no one thought they needed much in the way of formal schooling. They could be charming and attractive without that.

After the Revolution, during which LaFayette had fought skirmishes with the British near the Paynes' home, Dolly's father decided to make a change. Following the lead of other Quakers and of his own conscience, he freed his slaves, whom he had always treated kindly. Then, having sold his estate, he took his family to start a new life in the city of Philadelphia.

To the young girl from the country, Philadelphia was an exciting place. Wide-eyed, she listened to the crier call out the news on the street (although Philadelphia had a newspaper, many people still were unable to read). She heard endless political discussions, for the Confederation Congress held its sessions in the city.

Then, in 1787, came the Constitutional Convention, with great men from all the states but one taking part. Washington and Franklin were there; John Adams and Alexander Hamilton. James Madison, the brilliant student of government, was there too. Dolly must have heard of him, but their paths were not to cross until later.

In 1790, Dolly was a lively girl of twenty, dark-haired, blue-eyed. She was given in marriage to Quaker John Todd, a lawyer who may have been more her father's choice than her own. The Quaker wedding was simple and quiet.

Dolly Todd was happy, and she and John were soon the proud parents of two little boys. But in the summer of 1793, a yellow fever epidemic struck and carried off Dolly's husband and one of the little boys.

The sorrowing widow with the fatherless boy was still only twenty-five. It was small wonder that her undiminished charm and beauty continued to attract men to her. James Madison, now a representative from Virginia, was eager to meet her. Aaron Burr, who knew the Paynes, offered to introduce him. Soon, Madison, seventeen years Dolly's senior, was courting her insistently. Dolly was somewhat hesitant, considering the difference in their ages, but Martha Washington was said to have put in a good word for Madison.

So, in September, 1794, the two were married at the Virginia house of Dolly's sister, Lucy. In contrast to her first wedding, it was a grand occasion. There were feasting and laughter and music; they danced the minuet and the Virginia reel.

When the newlyweds set up housekeeping in Philadelphia, there began a gay social whirl. There were parties, receptions and balls, and everywhere Dolly was the merry and much admired center of attention. James Madison was a generous man and Dolly may have been somewhat extravagant. She loved to purchase beautiful and costly clothes, making her choices from dolls, dressed in the latest fashions, which were sent from Europe.

When Jefferson became President in 1801, he appointed Madison his Secretary of State. Since the President was a widower, Dolly often acted as his hostess for social occasions. Thus she added to her renown as the queen of capital society—now in the new city of Washington.

For one week every autumn, races were held in the new capital. During race week, Dolly, attracted by the excitement and color of the event, drove out in a coach drawn by four handsome horses. As always, attention focused on the lovely Mrs. Madison.

In 1804, Gilbert Stuart, the brilliant portrait artist, did pictures of the Madisons. Dolly liked that of her husband, but, womanlike, was not very enthusiastic about her own.

When Jefferson retired to Monticello in 1809, Madison succeeded him in the presidential office. The great social event that year was the first inaugural ball ever held. Elaborate preparations were made and four hundred guests attended. The new first lady was the belle of the ball. She wore a sleeveless yellow velvet gown, pearl necklace and bracelets, and a Paris turban. Dolly became known for her turbans, which she continued to wear even after they were no longer in style.

As the president's wife, Dolly gained new social laurels. Her interest in people grew and she became even more warmhearted and sympathetic. She seemed to be able to attract persons of all kinds and beliefs. Clever and tactful in her approach, she could talk awkward young men out of their shyness as well as she could impress diplomats and statesmen by her simplicity and graciousness.

Renowned for her dinner parties, where the tables fairly groaned with rich foods, Dolly is reported to have once served her guests an especially delicious dessert. When they demanded the name of this delicacy, their hostess told them it was *ice cream*. It was little known at that time.

Although Madison was a peace-loving man, the War of 1812 was fought while he was President. British interference with our shipping had grown outrageous and many of Madison's supporters were insistent on war, so Madison finally recommended that Congress make a war declaration against England.

Our tiny Navy scored some notable sea victories early in the war. The Navy Ball of December, 1812, afforded a stirring scene when a young naval officer presented Dolly Madison with the flag from a British vessel which had been captured by an American ship.

Later on, however, American arms met reverses. The British, following their victory at Bladensburg, only a few miles from Washington, marched on our capital. President Madison had to leave the city with some of his cabinet members. Dolly stayed behind long enough to pack and remove from the executive mansion some of the newer furnishings and the silver, and some important papers from the President's desk. A message came from the President, urging her to flee before the advancing Redcoats. But, at the last minute, exhibiting high courage and coolness, Dolly went back into the executive mansion to direct the removal of a historic portrait of George Washington from its frame. Only when she saw it safely driven away did the gallant lady consent to enter the horse-drawn coach for the dramatic dash to safety. The little Quaker girl had become the nation's heroine.

The British troops soon marched into the city and burned the Capitol building, the executive mansion and other public buildings. Then a violent storm arose, wind lashing trees and houses and a downpour quenching the fires. Disconcerted, the occupying army withdrew.

The Madisons returned in a few days, to grieve over the ruins. They went to live in a private home until the executive mansion, thereafter to be called the White House, had been rebuilt.

With the return of peace, the capital's social life was renewed and Dolly again assumed her place as the nation's hostess. A wonderful party was given for General Andrew Jackson, hero of the Battle of New Orleans.

In 1817, the Madisons left the White House to live a quiet life at Montpelier, their home in Virginia. The ex-President spent much time in his library, while Dolly's happiest hours were spent in her flower garden. They had great numbers of guests to entertain. In 1824, LaFayette, America's friend, visited them for several days. He, like all the others, was captivated by James Madison's wife.

After Madison's death, his widow moved to Washington, there to spend the remainder of her life. The two-story house on LaFayette Square in which she made her home still stands, and is called the Dolly Madison House. Her new home soon became one of the centers of the capital's social activity. Leading statesmen like Webster, Clay and John Quincy Adams often visited Dolly.

So the aging but still spirited lady found happiness in the society of old friends and the nation's newly great. She drew people to her like a magnet and gave them a chance to forget their worries and enjoy goodly company.

For some time she was hard-pressed by financial troubles. She refused to complain, and when friends discovered her poverty, they helped her out. Fortunately, her difficulties were solved in her last years by the sale of Montpelier and by Congress's purchase of James Madison's historically important papers.

The last public appearance of the grand old lady was at President Polk's reception in February, 1849. The President himself proudly offered his arm to smiling Dolly Madison.

Soon after that she was gone, although not from the hearts and memories of the American people. They could never forget the First Lady of the land who had so happily combined laughter and courage.

Paul Revere

The Man
Who Rode to Fame

THERE ARE few more exciting stories in American history than that of Paul Revere. The account of his ride through the night to call out the Minute Men and warn Massachusetts patriots against the British has thrilled young Americans for generations.

Paul Revere loved freedom above everything else. Even as a boy he had special appreciation of its importance, since his father had come from France to escape religious persecution.

Apollos Rivoire, Paul's father, had been sent to America by his own parents when he was only twelve years old. They were determined to get him away from the bad conditions in their own land. In America, he was apprenticed to a Boston goldsmith.

Apollos made many friends in Boston, but since all had trou-

ble pronouncing his name, he decided to change it to Paul Revere. When he was twenty-one years old he opened his own
shop as a gold- and silversmith and soon married. His third
child, Paul, was born January 1, 1735. As a child, the young
Paul heard time and time again the stories of his father's early
life, and grew up hating oppression and loving freedom.

He attended North Grammar School for several years and
then started to learn his father's trade. He soon showed unusual
skill as a silversmith and he is still remembered as one of the
most skillful craftsmen this country has ever had.

When Paul was twenty-two, he married Sarah Orne. Following his marriage, he began branching out in his business. He became a blacksmith as well as a silversmith. He also made
whistles and chains, sleigh bells and cowbells. He even made
false teeth, and it is said George Washington was once one of
his dental customers.

In 1765, when the hated Stamp Act was imposed upon the
colonies, Revere became a leader in an organization called the
Sons of Liberty. He helped patrol the streets, watching the
British, and when King George the Third sent troops to Boston,
he helped collect and hide arms and ammunition. He also
served as courier for the patriots, and in December, 1773, took
part in the Boston Tea Party.

Then came April 18, 1775. John Hancock and Samuel Adams,
two of Massachusetts' most important colonial leaders, were in
Lexington. It was suspected that the British were plotting to
take them prisoner and to seize munitions and supplies hidden
in Concord. Revere was told to be ready to ride with a warning, and around nine o'clock that night the message came—the
British were boarding ships to go to Lexington!

Putting on a dark cloak, Revere hurried away toward the
Charles River, his dog at his heels. Two friends were to row him
across, but as the trio neared their hidden boat, they realized

they had nothing with which to muffle the oars. Luckily a woman loyal to the colonists lived near by. The men called softly below her window, explaining their difficulty. A moment later a soft garment fluttered down to the ground. It was a flannel petticoat.

Then Revere suddenly realized he had forgotten his spurs, but again he quickly solved the problem. Writing the word "Spurs" on a slip of paper, he tied the note to his dog's collar and whispered a command. A few minutes later the dog was back with the spurs around his neck.

Out in the stream, British warships were anchored directly in the path their boat must take, but miraculously they crossed without being seen. Stepping ashore, Revere looked back at two lights gleaming in North Church tower. He had arranged for them to be hung as a signal to a substitute rider in case he was stopped: one lantern if the British took the land route; two, if they took the sea route.

A horse was ready for Revere who lost no time getting started. Off to Lexington he rode, stopping at every farmhouse along the way just long enough to pound on the door and shout the news of approaching danger. Drowsy farmer members of the patriot group called the Minute Men, jumped from their beds and hurried to Lexington. When the British arrived at dawn, they found sixty men lined up in the village square. A shot was fired and the Revolutionary War was on.

Later that same year, before becoming an officer in the Continental Army, Revere performed another great service for the Colonial cause. He was sent to Philadelphia to study the workings of the only powder mill in the Colonies. Although only allowed to pass through the building once, he was so quick and so accurate in his observations that he was able to set up a powder mill at Canton and supply the Colonies with desperately needed gunpowder. During the Revolution, he served as an officer in an artillery regiment.

When peace came he resumed his trade as a silversmith. He also established an iron foundry, made large bells and is said to have been the first manufacturer of copper sheeting in America.

On May 10, 1818, death came to bring to an end a useful and busy life.

Master Magician

HARRY HOUDINI did his first trick before an audience at the age of nine. He did his last, forty-three years later, a week before his death. In the years between, he amazed and delighted millions of showgoers in many countries.

As an escape artist, Harry Houdini topped them all. In fact, some of his feats were so baffling he·was often accused of having supernatural power. Houdini never revealed the secrets of his most famous escapes, but pointed out repeatedly that all were accomplished by natural means.

The great magician's success did not come easy. Perfecting each new trick meant weeks, sometimes months of practicing. Houdini had complete control over every muscle in his body. His feet were practically a second pair of hands.

Harry Houdini was born in Appleton, Wisconsin, on April 6, 1874, the fifth of eight children of Rabbi Mayer Samuel Weiss.

Originally named Erich Weiss, at sixteen he changed his name to Harry Houdini, after the French magician, Robert Houdin.

By the time Harry was seven he was earning his own way by peddling papers and blacking boots. He was also learning tricks. Whenever and wherever a magician performed in Appleton, there was little Harry, studying every move. Circus stunts intrigued him, too, and by the time he was nine he could pick up needles with his eyelids while hanging by his heels. This trick earned him his first public appearance. It was in a circus in Appleton in 1883.

At twelve Harry ran away from home, but several years later he rejoined his family who were then living in New York. All the time his knowledge of magic was growing, and by 1892 he was making professional appearances with his brother Theodore.

Two years later, following a whirlwind courtship, he was married to Beatrice Rahner. "Bess," as he always called her, then became his partner. Billed as "The Great Houdinis," they toured from town to town, playing in dime museums, medicine shows, fairs—wherever they could get an engagement. Their pay was seldom over twenty dollars a week.

Right from the start one of Houdini's best tricks was freeing himself from handcuffs. While working for an Appleton locksmith, he had made himself a tiny picklock and learned to pick all sorts of locks, handcuffs included. In 1898 he got a great idea to publicize this ability. Visiting the Chicago jail he had himself stripped naked, handcuffed and locked in a cell. In a few minutes' time, he had removed the handcuffs, unlocked the cell door, recovered his clothes and was greeting astonished reporters in the police chief's office. He repeated this stunt in many cities.

The Houdinis had their first real taste of success when given a season's booking on the Orpheum Circuit in 1899. Failing, however, to get hoped-for bookings at the season's end, Houdini decided to try his luck in London. There he became an instant hit after demonstrating his uncanny ability at Scotland Yard. The Superintendent himself had snapped England's newest type of handcuffs about Houdini's wrists, certain they could not be opened. But Houdini was free in a trice! All Europe proved equally enthusiastic, and so did the United States when the Houdinis returned in 1905.

By now the magician had streamlined his act to a few outstanding feats. One of these was swallowing a packet of needles and a length of thread, then drawing thread from his mouth with needles, all neatly threaded, dangling from it! Another stunt was his escape from a wooden box securely nailed about him by members of the audience. Later he proved himself just as clever at escaping from a coffin, a sealed paper bag, an iron boiler, a glass box and other containers.

For publicity purposes Houdini started making jumps from bridges while handcuffed. He would free himself underwater and reappear in a few seconds. One winter day in Detroit, however, Houdini had to make the leap through a large hole cut in the ice. Soon after hitting the water he had loosed the handcuffs, only to discover that the current had carried him under the ice. Through long training Houdini was able to go four minutes without drawing a fresh breath so he kept swimming around looking for the opening. One minute — two minutes — three minutes passed. Still nothing but ice was above him. Did he grow panicky? Not Houdini! But he had to have air. Then suddenly he remembered the tiny air space that exists between ice and water. This saved his life for he was able to get enough air to keep alive until a rope was tossed into the water. The rope caught his eye and guided him to the open air. He had been in the river eight minutes!

Wide publicity was also given Houdini when he had himself manacled and imprisoned in a wooden packing box weighted with lead. The box was then banded with steel and slid into New York harbor. It took Houdini just fifty-nine seconds to escape. On examination the box seemed untouched; his handcuffs and leg-irons were found inside.

Another of his hair-raising stunts was to escape from a strait jacket while suspended by his feet far above the street.

Many of Houdini's tricks were performed in full view of his audience. However, when he depended on the help of an instrument like the picklock, he would ask to be left alone or make use of a cabinet.

Houdini's favorite hobby was collecting data on magic—books, magazines, prints, clippings, playbills. Much of this material he utilized in writing *Miracle Mongers and Their Methods*, *The Unmasking of Robert Houdin* and other books. In connection with his crusade against fraudulent spiritualists, he wrote *A Magician Among the Spirits*.

Houdini died in Detroit on October 31, 1926. His extremely valuable collection of material on magic was willed to the Library of Congress.

Louisa May Alcott

Author of "Little Women"

WHEN THOMAS NILES, a Boston publisher, asked Louisa May Alcott to write a book for girls, Miss Alcott did not take him seriously. She felt sure she could not write anything girls would enjoy. A few months later the publisher asked her again. The Alcott family was greatly in need of money, so Louisa May decided she might as well try.

That was the beginning of *Little Women*—probably America's best-loved story for girls. Written in 1868, the book is still enormously popular. Readers today find Meg, Jo, Beth and Amy every bit as delightful as their grandmothers and great-grandmothers did.

However, back in the summer of 1868, the first few chapters did not seem at all promising to Mr. Niles. When the book was complete, he felt no better. Should he publish it? If it did not sell, he would lose a great deal of money. But Mr. Niles was a wise man. He decided to get the opinion of his teen-age niece.

"Oh, Uncle Tom, it's a wonderful book," she told him when she had finished. "I loved every word of it."

The publisher was surprised, but pleased, too. He showed the manuscript to a number of other girls. Each said the same: it was the best story she had ever read!

So Mr. Niles published the book. *Little Women* turned out to be the most successful book ever published by his firm.

The first part of the book ended with the engagement of Meg, but young America was not satisfied. "What happened to all the others?" they begged to know. Miss Alcott then wrote a sequel, and this was published early in 1869. The second part was received as enthusiastically as the first. The two parts are now usually published together and have been translated into many different languages.

After that Miss Alcott wrote many fascinating books for both boys and girls, each of them rousing a demand for more. The secret of her lasting appeal is probably that her books are peopled with boys and girls who act and think like real boys and girls.

Many of Miss Alcott's characters are taken from real life. Jo, for instance, is really the author herself. And Meg, Beth, and Amy closely resemble the three sisters she loved so much— Anna, Elizabeth and Abba May.

Louisa May Alcott was born on November 29, 1832, in Germantown, Pennsylvania. She was the daughter of Amos Bronson and Abigail May Alcott. Louisa's father was a schoolteacher, whose head was full of dreams. His teaching methods were far ahead of his time, but he was unappreciated and seldom made a large enough income to support his family.

It would be hard to imagine a family whose members were more devoted to each other than the Alcotts. In spite of being very poor most of the time, they found so much happiness in just being together that they never thought of feeling sorry for themselves.

When Louisa was two, the family moved to Boston. In those days the trip from New York to Boston was made by boat and on the way little Louisa decided to do a bit of exploring. An hour later her family found her—dirt and oil from head to foot, having a wonderful time in the engine room.

From their new home on Front Street in Boston, it was a short walk to Boston Common, and the Alcott children spent many hours there. One day Louisa fell into the frog pond, but a friendly little Negro boy quickly pulled her out. She was quite unhurt except for having a tummy full of pond water.

The move to Front Street in Boston was the first of many changes. By the time Louisa was twenty-six years old she had known some twenty different homes. Of all these places, her favorite was "Hillside," the big frame house in Concord where the family spent three happy years. Back of the house was a fine big barn—an ideal place to give plays. Louisa wrote the plays and made the costumes, and she and her sisters always took all the parts.

Ralph Waldo Emerson was also a resident of Concord and one of Bronson Alcott's closest friends. He became Louisa's good friend, too, and their friendship lasted throughout his whole life.

When Louisa was sixteen she wrote a series of charming little fables about birds and flowers for little Ellen Emerson. Ellen listened to them, wide-eyed and happy, but it didn't occur to the writer that others might be interested in these same little stories. Six years later, however, her father ran across one of the stories. He showed it to a publisher who not only bought the little story but published all the rest in a slender volume called "Flower Fables." Louisa's first book! How proud she was! It didn't matter to her that she received only thirty-two dollars in payment.

In December, 1862, Louisa left home to do volunteer duty in a Union hospital in Georgetown. There she worked as never before. Her patients were soldiers, some with typhoid and pneumonia, as well as the hundreds of wounded brought in from the battlefields. Besides nursing, she scrubbed and scoured, wrote letters for her patients and ran endless errands. Through it all she laughed and joked, but she was doing far more than her strength would allow. At the end of six weeks she was ordered to bed, desperately ill.

Louisa was sick for many months. Her father came and took her home to Concord, but it was May before she was downstairs at all. Before her illness Louisa's hair had been her great pride. Thick and dark, it reached almost to the floor. Now it was cut close to her head.

While in Georgetown, Louisa had written many colorful letters home about her hospital experiences. Parts of these letters were printed in a Boston paper under the title, "Hospital Sketches." Later they were reprinted in book form and brought Louisa her first real recognition as a writer.

Louisa made a trip to Europe in 1865 with an invalid friend. The trip wasn't all she had hoped for, since responsibility tied her down, but she made one splendid friend. This was a young Polish boy, Ladislas Wisinewski. They spent many happy hours together. Ladislas was the model for Laurie in *Little Women*, written two years after her return to America.

Long years before, Louisa had vowed that she was going to pay every family debt and provide her loved ones with every comfort. *Little Women* was the first big step toward making this possible. Then followed *An Old Fashioned Girl; Little Men*, written while in Europe with her sister May and a friend in 1870; a novel called *Work;* and several more charming books for young people.

As the author grew older, she grew more and more frail. Returning from a visit to her sick father in the spring of 1888, Miss Alcott became chilled and was taken ill. On March sixth, she died without knowing that her father had preceded her in death just two days before. She is buried in Sleepy Hollow Cemetery in Boston.

Samoset

Friendly Indian

ONE MARCH day in 1621 several Pilgrims at Plymouth, Massachusetts, were startled to see an Indian coming toward them from the woods. Ever since landing at Plymouth Rock in December, they had lived in fear of attack by the red men. The winter had been bitterly cold, they had been almost without food, and nearly half of the little settlement had died. Up till now no Indians had ever come close, but the Pilgrims had been afraid that they might grow bolder if they guessed how many deaths there had been. So as each was laid to rest, the ground over the grave was smoothed down carefully. There must be no telltale mounds to give away their sad plight.

The winter was over at last, but now came this Indian. What could he want? Tall and straight, he was completely naked except for moccasins and a strip of leather with a wide fringe which he wore about his waist. His hair hung long in back but was cut short in front. He had no bow and arrows and no tomahawk. Obviously he could mean no harm. Suddenly the brave raised his arm in salute and to the Pilgrims' utter amazement called out in English, "Welcome, Englishmen!"

After they had recovered enough to speak, the colonists welcomed their visitor and took him to the governor and Captain Miles Standish. It was easy to see that the Indian was hungry and cold, so the Englishmen immediately gave him food to eat and a coat to wear. As he ate, he told them about himself.

His name was Samoset, he said, and he had learned to speak English from Virginia settlers who had come north to fish. He was a Wampanoag Indian of the Pemaquid Territory. He came from Moratiggon, where he was a sagamore, or chief. To explain Moratiggon's location, Samoset pointed to the north, saying that it took five days to get there by land or one day by sea with a favorable wind.

When the Pilgrims asked the red man why they had seen so few of his people, their visitor explained that only a few years before a great plague had swept the vicinity. Indians had died by the hundreds. In one village only a single person had survived—a brave by the name of Squanto who also spoke English.

Samoset went on to say that Squanto had been carried off by an English sea captain when only twelve years old and had been sold into slavery across the sea. Taking pity on the unhappy Indian, some monks had paid for his freedom. Then a kind Englishman had paid for Squanto's passage back to America.

Samoset also told the Pilgrims about Massasoit. the great chief of all Wampanoags, and said both Squanto and Massasoit would call on them.

Not long afterward Squanto appeared. He became a scout

and interpreter for the English and proved of inestimable value. As a sign of friendship, Squanto brought the Pilgrims a little leather sack filled with seed corn, something they had never seen before. When the ground had been tilled the Indian showed them how to plant the corn, using small dead fish for fertilizer. He told them that corn must have plenty of sun and showed them how to kill the trees in the garden plot by cutting away bark just above the ground. He supplied them with seed for raising pumpkins and squash. He taught them to trap small animals with snares and to spear fish off Cape Cod.

One day Squanto came running into the village to announce that Massasoit was only a short distance away. Preparations to receive him were hastily made, and Captain Standish went out to meet the great chief. After exchanging greetings, Standish escorted the Indian and twenty of his braves to the village meeting house where the other colonial leaders had gathered. After Massasoit had been given a place of honor, food was brought in and there was "strong water" to drink.

When all had had their fill, the Englishmen and the chief smoked the calumet, or pipe of peace, and a treaty of friendship was made. This was the first treaty made between white men and red men in this country; it lasted throughout Massasoit's life.

By fall the Pilgrims were able to make a great harvest of the corn and other vegetables Squanto had helped them plant. They had gathered wild berries and fruits during the summer and had preserved great quantities for winter use. Venison and other game crowded the smoke houses. Wild turkeys and geese flew over the village every day.

Blessed by such abundance, the Pilgrims decided to have a great feast of thanksgiving, inviting all their Indian friends. Squanto sped from village to village with the invitation. Nothing could have pleased the Indians more. All accepted and on the day set, they appeared in their most colorful festival regalia. The feasting lasted three days with religious services twice a day.

After that Massasoit paid many visits to Plymouth. One of the last was made not long before his death in 1662. At that time he brought his two sons, whom the English called Alexander and Philip. He hoped that cordial relations might continue between them and the white men. But this was not to be, for it was Philip who became the Indians' leader in their last-ditch fight against the English in New England.

Squanto, unhappily, lived only about a year after the first Thanksgiving. On a trading trip down the coast, he became ill of fever and died at Chatham in 1622.

Samoset continued to be a regular caller at the Pilgrims' settlement and in 1624 told them proudly of the birth of a son. History also mentions that in 1625 he sold twelve thousand acres of Pemaquid territory to John Brown, an Englishman who had settled at New Harbor. This was the first deed made between an Englishman and Indians.

It is believed that Samoset died about the middle of the 1650's near Bristol, Maine. Helpful to the last, he had proved himself a true and honest friend of the Pilgrims.

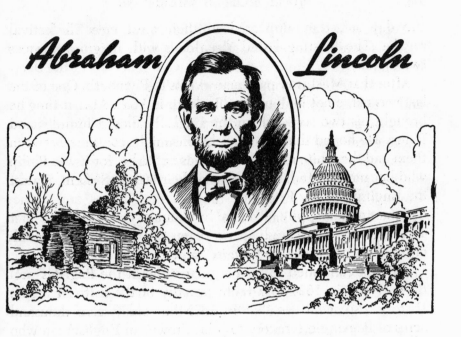

Abraham Lincoln

The Great Emancipator

AMONG AMERICAN patriots Abraham Lincoln stands shoulder to shoulder with George Washington. We honor Washington as the "Father of Our Country." We honor Lincoln as the savior of the Union, the man who prevented its division and ruin and brought freedom to all Americans.

At first glance Abraham Lincoln had little of the appearance one might expect in a man singled out by Fate to guide a nation through its greatest crisis. Six feet four inches tall, he was big-boned and awkward. His nose was large, his lower lip thick and protruding. His small gray eyes were deep-set beneath bushy, dark brows, and his generous ears flared from his head. His clothes hung loosely upon his frame, and the sleeves of his coat always appeared to be a little too short above his big hands.

189

Yet there was nobility in both his figure and face. The homely features seemed to express the depth and incorruptibility of his character. Wisdom and courage were reflected in the deep-furrowed face, also sympathy and kindness, tolerance, sincerity and steadfast good humor—all qualities the great man gave proof of possessing time and again as he raised himself from nothingness to worldwide and everlasting fame.

As every American knows, Abraham Lincoln was born in a log cabin. The date was February 12, 1809; the place, Hardin County, Kentucky. He was the son of Thomas and Nancy Hanks Lincoln. He had one sister, Sarah.

When Abraham was seven years old, the Lincoln family moved to Gentryville, Indiana, and during the first winter there they did not even have a cabin in which to live. Through bitter cold and raging snowstorms they huddled in a rude log shelter, closed on three sides only. Practically their only food was wild game and nuts.

Abraham's father loved his family, but he had little of the "get-up-and-go" of the true pioneer. He seldom worked harder than was absolutely necessary. Thus, the cabin he built the following summer had no floor or windows and only a flapping deerskin for a door. The children gathered leaves to make beds for themselves. Their parents' mattress was made of corn husks. As in all early American homes, meals were cooked in a big stone fireplace.

About a year later Mrs. Lincoln died. Life was lonely and hard without a mother in the home, and Thomas Lincoln soon remarried. His second wife, Sarah Bush Johnston, took to Abe immediately, and the boy liked her. Her influence on him as he grew to manhood could not have been better. Cheerful and kind, she was a sympathetic person who encouraged him in his love of reading, gave careful consideration to his every question, and quieted her husband's objections to Abe's going to school when he might have been working on the farm.

Without nagging, she got Tom Lincoln to do things he had been putting off for years. It wasn't long before the cabin had an oiled-paper window, a fine split log door and even a floor. Now, with the furniture and bedding she had brought from Kentucky, the cabin became a real home.

Abe was always the last to bed at night, for he read till the last bit of light from the fire was gone. Most of the books he borrowed from a lawyer in Rockport, seventeen miles away. Abe usually had to walk both ways, but he always considered the books more than worth the effort it took to get them.

In 1830 the family moved again, this time to Macon County, Illinois. Not long afterward Lincoln started clerking in a New Salem store. One day he discovered that a customer had given him six cents too much. The woman had already left the store, so at the end of the day, Lincoln walked to her home, five miles distant, to give her the six cents. Is it any wonder he was called "Honest Abe"?

During the next few years Lincoln studied law from borrowed books. He earned his living in various ways. Among other things he was hired to work on a flatboat running to New Orleans. There, seeing a slave auction, he declared, "If I ever get a chance to hit that thing, I'll hit it hard."

Lincoln held his first political position in 1834, when he was elected to the Illinois legislature. He served four consecutive terms. In 1837 he started practicing law and two years later opened an office in Springfield.

With the birth of the Republican party in 1854, Lincoln became its leader in Illinois. Then came the famous campaign of 1858, in which Lincoln and Stephen A. Douglas were candidates for the United States Senate. Touring the state together, they debated the election issues, first among which was the question of the extension of slavery to the United States Territories. Vigorously opposing this, Lincoln stated flatly, "A house divided against itself cannot stand. I believe this Government cannot endure permanently half slave and half free."

By his boldness, Lincoln lost the election, but his brilliant speeches focused the spotlight of national attention upon this man who dared to meet an issue squarely.

He became the Republican nominee for the presidency in 1860 and, though violently opposed by the South, was duly elected. However, between his election in November and his formal inauguration in March, seven southern states seceded from the Union. Soon afterward four more states withdrew. The Southern Confederacy was formed and on April fourth the first blow of the Civil War was struck when the South fired upon Fort Sumter.

During the next four years, Lincoln proved his greatness many times. A tower of strength, he led his people through the bitter period of war. Although weighted with problems, he somehow found time to perform many kindnesses. One of the small deeds that will always be remembered is his writing a personal letter to a mother who had lost five sons in battle.

From the start Lincoln's declared aim was to save the Union. He hated slavery but did not issue his Emancipation Proclamation until he felt that it must be done as a war measure. In September, 1862, he announced that all slaves would be freed in states still fighting on January 1, 1863. War continued as before and on the first day of 1863 four million slaves were declared free men.

With the victory at Gettysburg in July, 1863, the tide of war turned definitely in favor of the North. Four months later, when part of this battlefield was dedicated as a national cemetery, Lincoln was asked to say a few words although Edward Everett was the main speaker of the day. At the end of two hours, when Everett had finished, the president put aside

Lincoln Gave His Famous Speech at Gettysburg

his tall beaver hat, rose to his feet and quietly began, "Four score and seven years ago . . ."

There is no need to go on. The simple and beautiful words of his brief address are familiar to every American. They will live forever, an eloquent expression of Lincoln's great soul.

Another of his finest addresses was that delivered at his second inaugural, March 4, 1865, when he closed with these stirring words:

"With malice toward none; with charity for all; with firmness in the right, as God gives us to see the right, let us strive on to finish the work we are in; to bind up the nation's wounds; to care for him who shall have borne the battle, and for his widow, and his orphans—to do all which may achieve and cherish a just and lasting peace among ourselves, and with all nations."

On April ninth, General Robert E. Lee surrendered. The tired nation lay down its arms, and five days later the flag of the United States was again flying over Fort Sumter.

That evening, accompanied by his wife, Mary Todd Lincoln, and several friends, the president attended a comedy at Ford's Theater. As the group in the presidential box was absorbed in watching the action on the stage, the door opened behind them. Ever so quietly J. Wilkes Booth, an actor, stepped from the corridor into the box. Raising a gun he fired quickly. The nation's leader slumped in his chair. The following morning, April 15, 1865, Abraham Lincoln died. He is buried in Springfield, Illinois.

Booth believed the South had been wronged by Lincoln, but by assassinating him, the actor cut down the one man who might have been able to prevent the sorrowful conditions which prevailed in the South during the period of Reconstruction.

Luther Burbank

Plant Wizard

By WORKING "miracles" with flowers and fruits, Luther Burbank made America a lovelier and better place in which to live. Because of him hundreds of growing things have attained new beauty and perfection.

Burbank's wonders were achieved through hard work, study and unending experiment. Along with ingenuity and imagination, this great naturalist had infinite patience and keenest powers of observation. He could detect the slightest variation in the fragrance, color or size of a flower or fruit. Out of thousands he could pick the one plant that showed an improvement over all its fellows. From that one plant he could develop hundreds or millions of plants just like it.

In rare instances, a happy accident of nature helped him develop a new variety. But, in the great majority of cases, he guided nature by painstaking experiment involving the crossing of many, many plants.

195

Luther Burbank was born March 7, 1849, in Lancaster, Massachusetts, the thirteenth child of Samuel Burbank, farmer and brickmaker.

As soon as Luther could walk he followed his mother around her flower garden. She taught him to weed and to water the plants and to plant seeds and thin out the baby plants. In a few years he had a section of garden for his very own.

Besides tending his garden, young Luther had his share of the usual farm chores, but there was also time for play. Though extremely quiet and reserved with strangers, the boy had a good time with his family and close friends.

After attending the district school, Luther was sent to Lancaster Academy for four winters. The summer months he spent learning pattern-making at a plow works in Worcester. One winter a German scientist presented a series of lectures in Lancaster which interested young Burbank very much. However, he afterward said that the real turning point of his life was reached when he happened on to a copy of Charles Darwin's *Variations of Animals and Plants Under Domestication.* From then on, Burbank knew that pattern-making was not for him.

In 1871 the young man bought seventeen acres of land in Lunenburg with money left him by his father. Here he raised fine vegetables for the market and also began experimenting. Within a few years he had developed the new and better Burbank potato.

Burbank became very much interested in a Lunenburg girl. Downhearted when a misunderstanding arose between them, he decided to go to California as three of his brothers had already done. Needing money for the trip, he sold the rights to the Burbank potato to a seedsman for only one hundred and fifty dollars. The seedsman, however, allowed him to keep ten potatoes from which to grow more in California. By the time he reached the west coast, these potatoes were practically all the capital he had.

The town of Santa Rosa where Burbank settled is beautifully situated in a fertile valley north of San Francisco. Burbank liked the place instantly. No one could have written more glowing accounts of the Golden State than did this newcomer. In his frequent letters home, he told of squashes three and a half feet long, bunches of grapes half a yard long, cabbages as big as washtubs, rose trees thirty feet high, geraniums that grew like trees, the wonderful climate, the magnificent scenery. Is it any wonder his mother and a sister joined him in his new home two years later?

But for all the beauty about him, Burbank found the going hard for several years. Once, soon after his arrival, he cleaned a lot of hen houses, just to be able to sleep in a coop. Later he was pleased to get a job at a nursery, but it turned out that his sleeping quarters were over the greenhouse. Day and night his surroundings were close and humid. Never robust, he soon became ill and had to give up this work.

When he was well again he started his own small nursery. The first year his sales amounted to fifteen dollars and twenty cents. Ten years later, when he sold the nursery, sales topped sixteen thousand dollars.

Burbank gave up the nursery to spend all his time on experimentation. Previously he had had to spend most of his time filling specific orders. However, doing this successfully had often presented quite a challenge.

There was, for example, the time he received an order for twenty thousand prune trees of a certain size, to be delivered within a year. Burbank knew at once that it was impossible for prune trees to grow to the specified size in a year. Nevertheless, the order was ready in ample time. Instead of prune trees, Burbank had planted almond trees which grow very rapidly; to these he had later grafted prune cuttings. The purchaser was quite content, for though the trees were almond trees, the fruit they bore was prunes.

During the years that followed, Burbank experimented with thousands of plant varieties and grew millions of individual plants. He worked from thirty to forty years on some of his projects.

Burbank was especially interested in plums and prunes. Besides developing new varieties, he grew a plum that had no pit, and by crossing a plum with an apricot he made an entirely new fruit, the plumcot.

Berries were another of his favorites. He produced ten new varieties. He grew thornless blackberry vines, and amazed an already wondering world by raising a white blackberry.

He also originated several varieties of thornless cacti for feeding cattle in desert country; a fragrant calla lily; the lovely Shasta daisy; the Burbank cherry; and a great many other fruits, flowers and vegetables.

Few of Burbank's experiments were done "for fun," but occasionally he produced an amusing freak such as a half sweet and half sour apple.

Burbank loved his work. He was interested in the practical side of scientific advances, but said with his characteristic sincerity, "I shall be contented if because of me there shall be better fruits and fairer flowers."

Luther Burbank died on April 11, 1926, and is buried at his home in Santa Rosa, California.

Victor Herbert

Master of Melody

ONE OF America's greatest musical treasures is the host of enchanting melodies written by Victor Herbert. Though many of his charming operettas have been heard in American cities every season since they were first written, audiences seem never to tire of this fine composer's music.

Victor Herbert was born in Dublin, Ireland, on February 1, 1859, son of Edward Herbert. His mother was the daughter of Samuel Lover, famous Irish painter, novelist, musician and entertainer.

Three years after Victor's birth his father died, and the boy and his mother went to live with Mr. Lover in his new home near London. During the next four years Victor's life was full of music. His grandfather loved to sing old Irish folksongs to the child, and his mother was a fine pianist.

When Victor was seven Mrs. Herbert took him to Germany

199

to be educated. The boy was a good student but he liked out-door sports, too.

With her own love of music, Mrs. Herbert urged Victor to study some musical instrument, but he kept begging off. Then one day when he was about fourteen, the school band leader came to Victor in desperation. He needed a piccolo player for a performance just two weeks off—could Victor possibly help him out? That was a tall order—to learn to play an instrument well in only two weeks—but somehow the boy did it, piping away from morning till night.

Obviously he had far greater than ordinary talent, and soon started studying the cello. In a few years' time he had become an excellent musician and was playing with some of Europe's finest orchestras, including that of the waltz king, Johann Strauss.

While first cellist with the Stuttgart Court Opera orchestra, Herbert did his first composing. He had a good time in Stutt-gart, too, and seemed to go everywhere and know everyone.

Then one day he saw a new singer on the opera house stage. She was a beautiful woman with a beautiful voice. Her name was Therese Forster. In 1886 she and Herbert were married and they came to America.

During his first years here Herbert played with the Metro-politan Opera orchestra, the New York Philharmonic and other fine orchestras, and was acclaimed by many critics as the best cellist of his day.

But Herbert was to have many careers in one. Now he start-ed conducting and in 1893 became leader of one of America's most famous bands. Later he directed the Pittsburgh Sym-phony and after 1904, he had his own orchestra.

With the production of *Prince Ananias* in 1894, Victor Her-bert entered the field that was to gain him his greatest fame—light opera. In the next twenty-three years, he wrote about forty musical comedies and operettas, frequently working on several simultaneously. He had five grand pianos in his home, also a huge workshop with many desks scattered about.

Among his greatest hits were *Mlle. Modiste, The Red Mill, Naughty Marietta* and *The Fortune Teller.* Two of his most popular individual songs are *Kiss Me Again* and *A Kiss in the Dark.*

Herbert has been compared with Sir Arthur Sullivan of the English comic opera producing team, Gilbert and Sullivan. But unfortunately, Herbert never found his "Gilbert" to write words equal to his music in quality and appeal. Except in rare instances, the lyrics of his operettas are weak. One of his grand operas, *Natoma,* is among America's best, musically, but here again, the libretto is not good.

After World War I, operetta waned in popularity but Herbert continued to write individual numbers for the Ziegfield Follies and similar revues. He also wrote musical scores for several motion pictures.

Herbert thoroughly enjoyed his fame. He liked good living and having enough money to satisfy his desires. He loved good food, and never missed a meal. What's more, if he had anything to say about it, every meal was excellent. He liked having friends about him and was a witty and good-natured companion. As an orchestra leader, he expected hard work at rehearsals but realized there must be time for fun, too. As a result his men went out of their way to do things to please him—like wearing green ties on St. Patrick's Day.

On May 27, 1924, while working on a Follies number, Victor Herbert suddenly collapsed with a heart attack and died in a few moments. His death was mourned by lovers of music the world over.

U.S. Grant

The Soldier-President

WHEN ULYSSES S. GRANT was thirty-nine years old, most of his friends—and he had many—felt forced to admit that he was a failure. He had bungled a promising military career. He had had to give up a farm because of sickness. He had failed in several business ventures and finally had to appeal to his family to get a poorly paid job as a tanner's clerk. Everyone acknowledged that he tried very hard, but somehow success seemed just out of reach.

Four years later, as commander in chief of the Union forces, the so-called "failure" was being hailed as a hero throughout the North. He had proved his military genius time and again, and in his final victory over the gallant Robert E. Lee, he proved his greatness.

Grant became the man of the hour. The people of the United States elected him to the nation's highest office. Rulers of countries all over the world paid him homage. He reached the peak of fame, yet fundamentally he was little changed from the quiet, sensible, determined boy who grew up on an Ohio farm.

Ulysses Simpson Grant, eldest son of Jesse Root and Hannah Simpson Grant, was born at Point Pleasant, Ohio, on April 27, 1822, and was baptized as Hiram Ulysses Grant.

Yes, Hiram Ulysses was his correct name, but since he was always called Ulysses, the Congressman who appointed him to West Point supposed it to be his first name. In sending in the appointment he added the boy's mother's maiden name as a middle name. Thus Ulysses was enrolled at West Point as Ulysses Simpson Grant and he chose to retain this as his name.

Not long after Ulysses's birth his parents moved to Georgetown, Ohio, where his father went into business for himself as a tanner, besides operating a small farm. As the child grew older, school kept him busy during the winter, but during the summer he was expected to help his father. Ulysses thoroughly disliked his tannery chores, but being very fond of horses, liked working with them in the fields.

At ten, the boy was an expert rider, and his proudest moment came when he had earned enough money to buy a horse of his own.

In later years neighbors liked to tell of the time a circus performer offered a money prize to anyone who could ride a certain balky pony. Ulysses was only about twelve years old, but he had confidence in his own ability to handle any horse, so volunteered to try. The pony kicked and reared, but the boy stuck to his back like a leech and won the prize.

Jesse Grant was extremely proud of his eldest son and determined that he should have every advantage. He was naturally very happy, therefore, when Ulysses received an appointment to West Point Military Academy. The lad had no particular desire for a military career, but was glad to get away from the tannery.

At the academy, it didn't take long for his classmates to nickname him "United States" and "Uncle Sam" because of the initials under which he had been registered.

Grant made excellent grades in mathematics and engineering and could outride every other cadet. In his other subjects he was only fair and upon graduation in 1843 ranked twenty-first in a class of thirty-nine.

As a second lieutenant, Grant was assigned to service in St. Louis where he fell in love with Julia Dent. The young couple became engaged, but it was not until after he had served with distinction in the Mexican War that they were married.

In 1854 a series of unfortunate circumstances, involving alleged intemperance on the part of Grant, led to his resignation from the army.

Joining his wife and family in Missouri, Grant farmed until his health gave out, then held several positions in St. Louis. Finally the family moved to Galena, Illinois, where his father and brother now had a thriving leather business. Grant went to work for them as a clerk.

With the outbreak of the Civil War, Grant offered his services to the Union cause, but had difficulty securing an army appointment. After several months, however, he was made colonel of the Twenty-first Illinois Volunteers. By July, 1861, he was a brigadier-general and was given command of the Cairo, Illinois, district.

In February, 1862, Grant captured both Fort Henry and Fort Donelson, taking fourteen thousand men. Promoted to the rank of major general of volunteers, he became commander of the district of western Tennessee. His leadership prevented disastrous defeat in the Battle of Shiloh.

Vicksburg was Grant's next important objective and after a long and spectacular siege the city surrendered on July 4, 1863. More than thirty thousand men were captured and the North gained control of the entire Mississippi.

Following Vicksburg, Grant was commissioned a major general in the regular army. Then came the Battle of Lookout Mountain where he defeated General Braxton Bragg in one of the most brilliant tactical maneuvers of the war.

A few months later he was given command of all the northern armies. Now a lieutenant general, he turned his attention to the east where he engaged General Robert E. Lee in the bitter and bloody Battle of the Wilderness.

It was during this first fierce combat between the two great leaders that Grant declared, "I shall fight it out on this line if it takes all summer."

On April 9, 1865, Lee was finally forced to surrender at Appomattox Court House, Virginia. There, through his courtesy and kindly understanding, Grant did more to promote better feeling between the North and South than could have been accomplished by a delegation of diplomats. It was customary to ask for the sword of the defeated general, but Grant had too much respect for Lee to do this. Furthermore, he allowed the southerners to return home, telling them to keep their horses for the spring plowing. The long struggle was over at last.

In 1868 Grant was made a full general, a rank created especially for him by Congress. Later that year he was elected President of the United States.

His first term in office was marked by the passage of the Fifteenth amendment and settlement of the *Alabama* claims dispute. Following his re-election in 1872 a series of scandals broke out which involved high government officials. Completely honest himself, Grant could not believe that his friends would do any wrong and, because of his misplaced faith in them, prevented correction of conditions.

Upon his return to private life, Grant and his wife made a tour of the world. They were honored with wonderful parties and priceless gifts everywhere they went.

Back in the United States, Grant made a number of unsound investments and lost his entire fortune.

The former president was now more than sixty years old and had contracted an incurable disease which caused him great suffering. Determined, however, to provide for his family, he started writing his *Personal Memoirs*. As his illness advanced, it seemed impossible that he could continue, but the courageous man refused to give up. Finally the manuscript was complete and just four days later, on July 23, 1885, the tired writer died.

Ulysses S. Grant is buried in a monumental tomb overlooking the Hudson River in New York City.

Alexander Graham Bell

Inventor of the Telephone

A LUCKY accident gave Alexander Graham Bell the clue he needed to invent the telephone. But if Bell hadn't been a scientist with a very special background, the chances are the incident would have meant little or nothing to him.

Bell was a professor of vocal physiology and his chief interest was in helping the deaf and dumb. As it happens, this had also been the life work of both his father and grandfather before him. All three were scientists and had made a careful study of sound transmission and the human voice. Young Bell naturally benefited greatly from the knowledge and experience of the two older men.

While teaching in Boston University, Bell started experimenting with multiple telegraphy. He had been giving much thought to the possibility of transmitting the human voice by electricity and during these telegraphy experiments uncovered the clue that led him to success.

As he was working one day, a taut wire broke in two and Bell was amazed to note that the snapping sound was transmitted through another wire which had metal disks at either end. That was all there was to it, but it started Bell off on the experiments which finally gave us the telephone.

From then on Bell and Thomas A. Watson, his assistant, worked feverishly. They made several false starts, but in about a year their dream became reality—they had made an apparatus which would transmit the human voice over wires. Their crude instrument would look a poor thing beside the efficient telephones of today, but it was nothing less than a marvel then.

The first sentence was spoken over Bell's invention in 1876. It was "Mr. Watson, come here, I want you." A year later Watson in Boston, was shouting over a long-distance wire to Bell in New York. Transcontinental telephone calls became possible in 1915; and on March 7, 1926, fifty years to the day after Bell's patent was granted, the first call was made across the Atlantic from New York to London.

Bell exhibited his telephone at the Philadelphia Centennial in 1876. It proved a great attraction but everyone talked about it as an amusing toy rather than a practical means of communication. It took Bell two years to convince people that it was practical. During this time he visited many cities demonstrating his invention while Watson in Boston talked and often sang into the transmitter.

After 1878 the number of telephones in use grew by leaps and bounds. Bell's right to the patent was hotly contested, but the United States Supreme Court upheld his claims and he and his associates made a fortune. The young inventor was also given high honors by many different countries but nothing ever meant more to him than his American citizenship.

Alexander Graham Bell was born March 3, 1847, in Edinburgh, Scotland, second of the three sons of Alexander Melville Bell. Alexander was given his lessons at home by his mother until he was ten years old. Then he was sent to an academy and later to the Royal High School, Edinburgh University and the University of London.

As a boy Alexander showed a great deal of ingenuity and was forever inventing some new and unusual game or activity. One of these was a "Fine Arts" society with various boy members taking turns giving lectures. Anatomy was Alexander's favorite subject and, using all the big words he knew, he would go on at a great rate while dissecting a dead bird or rabbit to give the lecture a really "scientific" touch.

As he grew older, he put his ingenuity to work at more useful things and while still in high school invented a mechanical device for husking wheat.

Both Alexander's brothers died from tuberculosis during the late 1860's and since Alexander's health was also poor, the Bells moved to Ontario, Canada, in 1870.

When his health improved the young man traveled to the United States where he gave special instruction to teachers of deaf mutes. In 1873 he joined the faculty of Boston University, and it was there that the accident that led to the invention of the telephone occurred.

Although Bell is famous for the telephone, he has other important inventions to his credit, including one of particular value in time of war; the telephone probe, an instrument with which a bullet or shell fragment in a body can be located without pain to the patient. Bell also continued his great work in furthering the education of the deaf.

Alexander Graham Bell died on August 2, 1922, while on vacation at his summer home in Nova Scotia. At the time of his burial, every telephone in North America remained silent as a tribute to the inventor.

Benjamin Franklin

Scientist, Philosopher and Statesman

AMONG ALL famous Americans, there is none more remarkable than Benjamin Franklin. He often accomplished more in a year than most men do in a lifetime, and everything he did, he did well.

As a representative of colonial America in the courts of Europe, he matched words and wits with the shrewdest diplomats of the time and seldom came off second best.

As a philosopher and writer, he was known throughout the colonies, and scores of his common-sense sayings are still part of our everyday language.

As a scientist he made one of the most important discoveries of his time—that electricity and lightning are one and the same—and his lesser discoveries and inventions would make a very long list indeed.

Benjamin Franklin was born on January 17, 1706, third youngest of Josiah Franklin's seventeen children. Josiah had come to Amercia about 1685. In England he had been a silk dyer but, finding little call for this trade in Boston, he became a tallow chandler and soapmaker. A tallow chandler made candles, a very essential business in those days, since there was no gas or electricity.

Even as a boy, Franklin was full of ideas for new ways to do things, and one of these ideas was soon copied by all his friends.

It happened this way. Near Franklin's boyhood home in Boston, Massachusetts, was a pond where he and his friends spent many happy hours, swimming and fishing for minnows.

Kite-flying was a favorite pastime, too, and one day Ben had his big idea. Why not put the two together? No sooner said than done. Into the water he went, tied the kite string around his waist, and in a jiffy was sailing away on his back, the wind in the kite drawing him across the pond.

Benjamin learned to read when he was very young, but didn't go to school until he was eight years old, and then only for two years. As a lad of ten he was put to work helping his father, but he hated the tallow business. Realizing this, Josiah Franklin soon arranged for him to become an apprentice in the printing shop of his half-brother, James.

James often treated him harshly, but Franklin worked hard and learned his trade well. Every spare moment he had he spent in reading and studying, and he also listened carefully to the many political discussions that took place in the shop. Soon he started writing articles voicing his own opinions. These he slipped under the door of the shop at night and, because they were very good articles, James printed them, although he did not learn for several months who had written them.

Franklin, however, was never happy in his brother's shop. He wanted to leave, but James refused to release him. After working for his brother for five years, he ran away to Philadelphia.

How tired he was when he arrived! And how hungry! His first move was to buy three big bread rolls. Tucking one under each arm, he started down the street munching the third. Poor hungry Ben! He must have presented a very funny sight. At least one charming young girl thought so. She laughed gaily as he passed her home, but waved a friendly hand, too. Her name was Deborah Read and seven years later in 1730, she became Benjamin Franklin's wife.

From Philadelphia, Franklin went to England but returned again after two years.

Three years later he bought his first newspaper and soon became known as a fearless publisher who always printed the truth.

The first annual edition of his *Poor Richard's Almanac* appeared in 1732. It immediately became very popular and was continued for twenty-five years. People still quote from it today. *You* do too, when you say, "Early to bed and early to rise makes a man healthy, wealthy and wise," or "God helps them that help themselves." Franklin wrote hundreds of such bits of advice. He was a firm believer in the virtues of industry, thrift and economy.

As Philadelphia's outstanding leader, he organized the police and fire-fighters, made the upkeep of streets a city function, founded the first public library in America, and served as postmaster general.

Intensely interested in science, he conducted many experiments and became convinced that lightning was electricity. To prove it, he made a special kite of thin silk and fastened a key to the kite string. He then flew the kite during a thunderstorm, and when he touched the key, sparks flew. Here was his proof —and Franklin put it to good use for all the world by inventing

Franklin Spent Some Time at the French Court

the lightning rod.

The Franklin stove was just one of many other inventions of this man. He never obtained copyrights or patents for his writings and inventions but gave freely of his time and effort for the common good.

Franklin's career as a diplomat and statesman began at the age of fifty-one, when he was sent to England to represent the colony of Pennsylvania. During a second period there, he was instrumental in bringing about the repeal of the Stamp Act and, by 1770, was representing not only Pennsylvania but Georgia, New Jersey and Massachusetts as well. In 1775, realizing that war between England and the colonies was inevitable, he returned to America.

After helping outline the Declaration of Independence, Franklin was among the signers on July 4, 1776. It was a serious moment, but even here Franklin's ready wit was in evidence.

When all had signed, John Hancock, president of the Continental Congress, said, "And now we must all hang together."

"Yes, John," said Franklin, "we must hang together or we shall all hang separately."

Shortly afterward Congress sent Franklin to France, where he obtained financial backing for the colonies in their fight against England. He remained abroad until after the peace was signed in 1783.

Upon his return home in 1785, he was elected president of Pennsylvania's executive council and served three one-year terms. During this time he was a delegate to the convention which framed the United States Constitution and was among the signers.

On April 17, 1790 the great man died at his home in Philadelphia. He was deeply and sincerely mourned, and the many services he performed through common sense, wit, diplomacy and experiment remain as a lasting memorial to his greatness.

Henry Wadsworth Longfellow

America's Favorite Poet

WHEN HENRY WADSWORTH LONGFEL-LOW was thirteen years old, he had his first poem published. What a thrill it was to see his own words in print and to hear his mother say it was a fine piece of work for a boy his age.

Henry adored his mother. He loved his father deeply, too, but Stephen Longfellow tended to be sterner than his joyous, lovely wife, who was full of encouragement for her son's literary ambitions.

With his seven brothers and sister, Henry grew up in the first brick house built in Portland, Maine. It was three stories high and had been erected by Mrs. Longfellow's father, General Peleg Wadsworth, who imported the brick from England. The General presented the place to his daughter shortly after

215

Henry's birth on February 27, 1807, and he himself went to live on his farm at Hiram, Maine.

How Henry did love to visit Grandfather Wadsworth! And Grandfather Longfellow, too, at *his* home in Gorham. He would tramp through the fields, gather berries and help around the barns. And at Gorham there were two special attractions—a place to swim and a blacksmith to watch at his work.

At home, too, happiness prevailed. In the evenings there would be singing round the harpsichord—or dancing, with laughter ringing through the rooms.

Young Henry was an excellent student. He read a great deal and Washington Irving's *Sketch Book* was his favorite. Though he was by nature a shy and gentle boy, he had a firm will of his own.

At fifteen he entered Bowdoin College as a sophomore. Writing verse was still a favorite pastime, and by the time he was a senior he had had a number of poems published.

His father opposed Henry in his desire to follow a literary career, but finally relented when Bowdoin offered the youth a professorship at the age of eighteen.

To complete his preparation for this position, Longfellow spent three years studying in Europe. In 1829 he returned to the college as professor and librarian with an annual salary of nine hundred dollars.

Two years later the young professor met and married Mary Potter, a pretty Portland girl.

In 1835, having been offered a professorship by Harvard University, Longfellow again went abroad to improve his German and to learn Swedish. He took Mary with him, but in Europe great unhappiness lay in store for him. Their first child was born, but died immediately, and a few weeks later Mary passed away, too.

Longfellow was heartbroken but forced himself to continue

his studies and the following year began his work at Harvard. Here he engaged rooms in Craigie House, General George Washington's headquarters while in Cambridge.

Life was pleasant at the University. Longfellow's teaching schedule was heavy, but he found time for his writing and made many new friends.

As a young man and throughout his lifetime, Longfellow was charming and gracious in manner. He was extremely neat and well groomed, with a carefully chosen wardrobe. He was, in fact, something of a dandy.

With the publication of his "Psalm of Life" in 1838, Longfellow began his real career as a poet. He next wrote the first of his famous American ballads, "The Wreck of the *Hesperus*," which is based on the story of a real schooner. His first book of poems appeared in 1839. Soon afterward came "The Village Blacksmith."

After a long courtship, he was again happily married in 1843 to Frances Elizabeth Appleton. Craigie House was a wedding gift from the bride's father, and there their six children were born. The names of the three youngest are familiar to all who have read "The Children's Hour": "Grave Alice and laughing Allegra and Edith with golden hair."

When he was forty-five, Longfellow finally gave up teaching to devote all his time to writing. At long last he had time for further study of the Indian legends and colonial history in which he was so interested. Soon new poetry began to flow from his pen. A year later "Hiawatha" appeared and in 1858, "The Courtship of Miles Standish." Nearly every boy and girl in America has read the romance of John Alden and Priscilla, but how many know that Alden was an ancestor of the author?

In the years following, many honors were paid Longfellow. While on a tour of Europe in 1867-68 Queen Victoria invited him to call; Cambridge and Oxford Universities gave him honorary degrees; he was received by important people everywhere.

At home admirers flocked to his home. Children came, too, many of them, and Longfellow loved their visits.

On his seventy-second birthday he received a very special present—an armchair made of wood from the selfsame chestnut tree about which he wrote in "The Village Blacksmith." Seven hundred school children each contributed a dime to help buy it for him.

Longfellow died March 24, 1882, and was mourned throughout the world. Two years later, his bust was placed in the Poets' Corner in Westminster Abbey, London. He was the first American to be given this honor.

Clara Barton

Lady of Mercy

BECAUSE SHE brought the Red Cross to America, Clara Barton's name will live as long as there is suffering, either from wars or natural catastrophes, such as floods and earthquakes.

Clara Barton was a little woman and not very pretty, but she had an air of strength and resolution that commanded respect. She worked like a Trojan to help anyone in need. She was courageous, sympathetic, and self-reliant. She showed a great deal of executive ability but found it hard to take criticism.

Born December 25, 1821, on a farm near Oxford, Massachusetts, Clara Barton was a Christmas present to her parents. Her father, Stephen Barton, was fairly well-to-do although the family always lived very simply. The new baby, youngest of five children, was named Clarissa Harlowe, after the heroine of a novel, but she was never called anything but Clara.

As a child, Clara was badly spoiled. Her brothers and sisters

219

were all much older than she, and they loved to fuss over their little sister.

Her father spent a great deal of time with Clara, too. He had served in the Indian Wars under daring "Mad Anthony" Wayne and told her many stories about his battle experiences.

Clara was a very smart little girl, but extremely shy. At school, even when she knew her lessons thoroughly, she could seldom bring herself to recite.

But while Clara was shy, she did not lack courage. Her brother David taught her to ride bareback when she was only five years old. When she was ten she often crossed the river at the sawmill by springing from one floating log to another.

The year Clara was eleven, David, always her favorite brother, was seriously injured in a fall. Clara insisted on acting as his nurse and for two years scarcely left the sick room. Not until her patient was well again did the family realize that too much work and too little sunshine had harmed Clara. She grew no taller from that time and was a mite of a thing all her life— hardly five feet tall and less than a hundred pounds in weight.

She was also shyer than ever, and her worried family finally consulted a phrenologist. Whatever the phrenologist may or may not have been able to tell from the shape of Clara's skull, he proved to be a wise and observant man. It was at his suggestion that she started teaching school, and in this work she gained self-confidence.

The phrenologist had also predicted that Clara would never hesitate to assert herself for others even though she might fail to do so for herself. The first time she showed how right he was, was in 1852 at Bordentown, New Jersey, where there was no free school. Determined that every child, poor or rich, should have the opportunity to get an education, Miss Barton set about establishing a public school, offering her services free for three months. Against much opposition, Miss Barton made a wonderful success where several others had failed completely. Starting with six pupils, she soon had six hundred.

At the end of two years Bordentown officials decided a man ought to head their flourishing school. They expected Miss Barton to be satisfied with stepping down to the assistant's job in the school she had created. They didn't know Clara Barton. Indignantly she resigned and went to Washington, D.C.

At the outbreak of the Civil War, the little independent set to work helping do good among the wounded troops who passed through the city. By advertising in several newspapers she obtained great quantities of food and other supplies to distribute among them.

In those days there were no women nurses or canteen workers at the front. After a few months' time, however, Miss Barton realized her work was needed among the soldiers and she made up her mind to get to the battlefields. This was easier said than done, but she finally got the necessary permission.

From then on Clara Barton was everywhere where there was fighting—helping to wash and dress wounds, preparing foods, comforting the dying.

At the close of the war Miss Barton continued her good work as head of the bureau of missing men, tracing thirty thousand soldiers, living and dead.

In 1869, she went to Switzerland for a long rest. There she heard for the first time about the International Red Cross. Dedicated to the relief of war wounded, the organization had been formed at Geneva, Switzerland, in 1863. Miss Barton learned to her surprise that all nations except the United States were members.

After working for a time with the International Red Cross in Europe during the Franco-Prussian War, Miss Barton returned to the United States. Again she was determined—this time to get her country to become a part of this organization of mercy.

For years Washington turned a deaf ear to her pleas, but Miss Barton refused to give up. When a devastating forest fire swept through Michigan she organized an American Red Cross Society to aid the victims. This showed the country that the Red Cross could be useful not only in international crises, but in local catastrophes, too. In 1882 the International Red Cross treaty was finally ratified.

Miss Barton became first president of the American Red Cross and served in this capacity until her resignation in 1904. As president, she attended many international conferences and supervised relief activities in the Jamestown and Galveston flood areas, in the Russian famine of 1892, in the Armenian massacres of 1896 and in Cuba during the Spanish-American war.

Clara Barton died at the age of ninety-one at her home near Washington, on April 12, 1912. She is buried at Oxford, Massachusetts.

Robert Fulton

Artist, Patriot and Inventor

TODAY, GIANT steamships cross the Atlantic ocean in less than five days. Early in the nineteenth century, the same trip took a month or more. In those days, ocean-going vessels had huge sails and depended on the wind to carry them from port to port. As for river boats, they were cumbersome, flat-bottomed affairs which carried cargo and occasional passengers. No one in a hurry used these boats. Going downstream, they depended on the current to carry them along, and going upstream, men had to force them along with poles.

Then, on August 17, 1807, a new kind of river boat was tested—an amazing boat with paddle wheels and a steam engine. It was Robert Fulton's _Clermont,_ and no shipbuilder was ever more nervous before a trial run. People crowded the shore, laughing and talking about "Fulton's Folly." They had come to make fun of this "crazy invention," but they stayed to cheer the anxious inventor.

To the crowd's astonishment the *Clermont* moved! True, it stopped a short distance from the pier, but in a little while it started again. Off to Albany! The one hundred fifty mile run from New York to Albany took thirty-two hours up the river and thirty hours back. Smoke and sparks poured from the tall smokestack; the big paddle wheels churned dizzily; and aboard the boat, friends clasped Fulton's hand, congratulating him over and over again. Wonderingly, they talked of what it all might bring, but probably few realized that Fulton's perfection of the steamboat actually marked the greatest advance in navigation since the first boat was launched. Others had experimented with steamboats, but Fulton was the first to build a really successful one.

Born on November 14, 1765, in Lancaster County, Pennsylvania, Robert Fulton was the son of Irish immigrants.

His father, a tailor, died when Robert was only three years old. His mother, left with five children to support, taught them their three R's and managed to send Robert to school when he was eight. He was a fair student, but was more interested in drawing, painting and making things than in books.

When only nine years old Robert hammered a lead pencil out of a scrap of the metal given him by a local gunsmith. He became so interested in the pencil he was late for school, but his handiwork made such an impression that his teacher let him off without punishment.

Several years later he got hold of some gunpowder and made pasteboard rockets to celebrate the Fourth of July. Nothing like them had been seen in Lancaster before.

Another of his boyhood inventions showed an early interest in boats. He and his friends often went fishing on the Conestoga

River. It was great sport, all except poling the heavy boat. Robert started experimenting and soon made a set of paddle wheels, turned by a crank. With these attached to the boat, no poling was necessary and fishing was far more fun for them all.

At seventeen, young Fulton left home for Philadelphia where he made a fair success as a painter of miniature portraits. During his spare time he drew patterns and plans for local manufacturers, and by the time he was twenty-one he had saved enough money to realize two ambitions. He bought a farm for his mother and a ticket to Europe for himself.

It was Benjamin Franklin who first urged Fulton to go to London to study art. The young painter had done a portrait of the statesman and had aroused Franklin's interest with his talent, hard work and thriftiness. Franklin gave Fulton a letter of introduction to Benjamin West, an American painter in London.

The next years were hard ones for Fulton. He arrived in England with only two hundred dollars and this soon went for tuition, art supplies, food and lodging. Four long years passed before he began to earn money enough to live comfortably.

Then suddenly in 1793, he decided to give up painting and turn to engineering. This decision was probably influenced by two important men he had met through West—one, the Duke of Bridgewater, founder of Great Britain's canal system, and the other, James Watt, celebrated inventor who had perfected the steam engine.

Fulton studied machinery in Birmingham, an important English industrial center, and soon took out patents on a number of inventions. These included a mill for sawing marble, a machine for spinning flax, another for making rope, and one for dredging canals.

In 1797 he went to France where he invented a submarine and a torpedo boat. Napoleon appointed a commission to examine this strange "plunging boat" but took no further action.

About this time Fulton's interest in steamboats was aroused by a meeting with Robert R. Livingston, American minister to France, who held exclusive rights to operate steamboats on all waters of New York state. Livingston was convinced a successful steamboat could be built and offered to finance the inventor's experiments.

Fulton's first steamboat was launched on the Seine river in 1803 but it broke in two and sank because the machinery was too heavy. Four months later his second steamboat was safely launched. It traveled against the current at a speed of about five miles an hour.

Throughout his years in Europe, Fulton had kept in close touch with the United States, making reports of his inventions to George Washington and others so that his own country might profit by them. Now that success of his steamboat seemed assured, Fulton returned to the United States to build the *Clermont,* installing in her a specially designed engine built in England by Watt.

The year following the boat's first trip on the Hudson, Fulton married his partner's daughter, Harriet Livingston.

During the next seven years, Fulton made a fortune by building steamboats for use on American rivers. His career was cut short at its height, however, when he caught a severe cold which led to complications causing his death on February 24, 1815. He is buried in New York's Trinity churchyard.

Harriet Beecher Stowe

Her Pen Was Mighty

IN DECEMBER of 1862, Harriet Beecher Stowe met Abraham Lincoln for the first time. As the president stretched out his hand in greeting, his first words were: "So this is the little woman who wrote the book that made this big war!"

The book to which Lincoln referred was *Uncle Tom's Cabin* and there was more than a little truth in his words. Mrs. Stowe's simple story of slavery in the South *did* help bring on the Civil War. First published as a magazine serial in 1851-52, the story stirred up more antislavery feeling than all other anti-slave speeches and articles put together. Everybody, everywhere talked about it. Southerners were apt to call it "a tissue of lies," while northerners praised it to the skies.

Although not a member of the Abolitionist party, Harriet Beecher Stowe had had a horror of slavery since she first heard it discussed as a child. Later, while living in Cincinnati, she had visited slave-holding plantations in Kentucky and during this same period had helped a number of runaway slaves reach Canada.

Many of the characters in her famous book were based on real people. Uncle Tom, for example, was inspired by a kindly Negro preacher, a former slave, whom she herself met. Simon Legree was modeled after a man her brother Charles had seen in the South. Within Charles's hearing the man had boasted that his fist had grown so big and hard from "knocking down niggers."

One of the writer's New England sisters-in-law was particularly bitter against slavery, and it was her urging which finally set Mrs. Stowe to work.

In the spring of 1851 she began her book, never dreaming that it was to become the most talked-of book of the times, that its total sale would run into the millions, or that it would eventually be translated into thirty-seven languages and dialects.

To say that Mrs. Stowe wrote under difficulties is putting it mildly. With seven children to care for, interruptions were constant. Some chapters were written in the kitchen while directing the work of the hired girl; others were done late at night.

Mrs. Stowe received three hundred dollars for her serial manuscript. For the book rights, she was paid a ten per cent royalty on every copy sold, which amounted to ten thousand dollars for the first three months alone. *Uncle Tom's Cabin* was also dramatized and played throughout the country, but Mrs. Stowe was never paid anything for the dramatic rights.

Harriet Beecher Stowe was born in Litchfield, Connecticut, on June 14, 1811, the daughter of the Reverend Lyman Beecher. Harriet's mother died when she was four years old. Two years later her father remarried. After that five new brothers and sisters were born, making fourteen little Beechers in all.

Of them all, Harriet's favorite companion was her younger brother, Henry Ward, who later became the most famous of the six Beecher boys entering the ministry.

At thirteen, Harriet was sent to Hartford to attend her sister Catherine's school and a year later was teaching part time herself. When the family moved to Cincinnati, Catherine opened a new school where Harriet taught until her marriage to Calvin Ellis Stowe in 1836. A great scholar, Mr. Stowe was a professor in the seminary headed by Harriet's father.

Writing interested Harriet from childhood and at twelve she composed an essay on the profound subject "Can the Immortality of the Soul Be Proved by the Light of Nature?" Among her first adult writings was a geography. She sold quite a number of manuscripts before starting *Uncle Tom's Cabin, or Life Among the Lowly*. She wrote thirty-three books in all, including *Dred, The Minister's Wooing* and *Old Town Folks*.

Harriet Beecher Stowe died on July 1, 1896, at the age of eighty-five. Because the greater part of her huge earnings had been poorly invested or given away, she left only a very small estate.

Franklin D. Roosevelt

Crisis President

ONE DAY in the 1880's, a proud father brought his five-year old son to call on President Cleveland. During the visit, the President patted the boy's head and said, "I'm making a strange wish for you, little man—I hope you will never be President of the United States."

President Cleveland's wish was not to come true, however. The boy was Franklin D. Roosevelt and he was elected president not once, but four times. He became one of the greatest leaders in our history.

Franklin Delano Roosevelt, the son of James and Sara Delano Roosevelt, was born at Hyde Park, Dutchess County, New York, on January 30, 1882. He was descended from Claes van Rosenvelt and Philippe de la Noye, both of whom came to America from Holland in the early 1600's.

During his boyhood at Hyde Park, Franklin Roosevelt learned

230

to ride, swim, sail and enjoy many other sports. He also developed several hobbies, notably that of collecting stamps. Starting when he was nine years old, he continued to collect stamps throughout his life. By the time he was in the White House he was the proud owner of thirty thousand stamps.

Liking anything that had to do with the sea, he also had a life-long interest in ship models. As a boy, he made many of his own. He read hundreds of sea stories and soon knew the life-history of every important naval hero. He started a collection of books about our Navy, which eventually became one of the world's finest on that subject.

Naturally, Franklin Roosevelt wanted to enter the United States Naval Academy. After consulting with his father, however, it was decided that he should carry on his father's varied business interests and that Harvard would give him a better background for that purpose. So he gave up the idea of a Navy career, although he never gave up his keen interest in naval affairs.

To prepare for Harvard, Franklin entered Groton School in Massachusetts. There he went out for various sports, establishing a record for the running high kick. His greatest scholastic achievement was the winning of the Latin prize in his senior year.

At Harvard, he was popular with both students and faculty, although he was not a brilliant scholar. By the time he was a senior, he was keeping steady company with Eleanor Roosevelt, a distant cousin of his, and shortly after his graduation their engagement was announced.

The two were married on St. Patrick's Day, 1905. President Theodore Roosevelt, Eleanor's uncle, gave the bride in marriage. There were three hundred guests, and thousands of other people waited outside to catch a glimpse of the famous "Teddy."

Since Franklin was still studying law at Columbia, their European honeymoon was postponed until the summer. In the fall, they returned to live in New York. A year later, Roosevelt started practicing law.

As their family grew in numbers, the Roosevelts came to spend more time at Hyde Park. Since 1900, when his father died, Franklin had to supervise all activities at the estate.

In 1910, the Democrats of Dutchess County persuaded Roosevelt to run for state senator. No one gave him a chance to win in that normally Republican district. However, determined to make a fight of it, he toured the countryside in a little red auto, carrying his campaign to the people in a way which forecast his later political methods. It proved effective, and he won the election by a good majority.

In the New York Senate, he led a successful fight against Tammany Hall and worked with other liberals for reform measures.

As a reward for his hard work in behalf of Woodrow Wilson in the 1912 presidential campaign, Roosevelt was made Assistant Secretary of the Navy the following year. This post he filled efficiently until 1920, when the Democrats nominated him for vice-president. However, it was not a Democratic year and, after the election, Roosevelt returned to his law practice.

In August, 1921, he went to join Mrs. Roosevelt and their five children at Campobello, New Brunswick, for a vacation. By way of celebration, there was a picnic party, followed by a plunge in the cold water of the bay. Roosevelt was chilled, developed a cold and, two days later, he was paralyzed from the hips down. He was a victim of infantile paralysis.

Those who took it for granted that Franklin Roosevelt's active life was over simply did not know the man. Determined to regain the use of his legs, he began that long struggle, at first apparently hopeless, which most Americans now know so well. It may have been those long, weary months of pain and stubborn effort which developed in Franklin Roosevelt the courage and will and faith which in later years stood him and the American people in such good stead.

For three years, he exercised and took treatments without making much progress. Then he heard of Warm Springs, Georgia, and went there without delay. He stayed in the warm pool for hours, making up his own underwater exercises. After a few weeks, he noticed a decided improvement.

Roosevelt went back to Warm Springs every year, and by 1928 he was so much better that he could walk with braces. To express his gratitude and to help other victims of infantile paralysis, he established the Warm Springs Foundation. He even built a small home there, where he spent much time encouraging and helping the patients.

Delegates to the 1928 Democratic Convention, where Roosevelt made a nominating speech for Al Smith, were surprised to see him so strong and healthy. On the insistence of Smith, he consented to run for governor of New York that year, and he won a surprising victory. He was re-elected in 1930.

In 1932, the American people were sick of depression and unemployment. They wanted a change. Franklin Roosevelt, the Democratic candidate for the presidency, promised them many changes. The people elected him and, once in the White House, he began to make good his promises.

When Roosevelt took office, the country was on the verge of disaster. Millions were out of work. Banks were failing. The prices of farm products were pitifully low, and farmers were losing their farms. The American people were afraid. They had almost lost faith in our democracy.

Then there came from the White House, calming, confident words: "This great nation will endure as it has endured, will revive and will prosper. . . . The only thing we have to fear is fear itself."

The words were followed by swift, spirited action, intended to pull the country out of the depression and to reform our economic system. The banks were closed by presidential order, to be reopened after careful examination. A special session of Congress, called by the President, passed various laws which he suggested, aimed at business revival and reform. They included industrial recovery, raising of farm prices, conservation of resources, changes in the system of credit and banking, and assistance to labor. Later on during Roosevelt's occupancy of the White House, Congress added laws on social security, collective bargaining by unions, and wages and hours.

Many people thought the "New Deal" went too fast and too far. Others gave it their fervent support. Even the experts could not agree. But apparently, the people as a whole approved, judging from Roosevelt's triumphant re-election in 1936, when he lost only two states

It is true that millions of people felt close to Franklin Roosevelt. He seemed to understand their problems and to be concerned for their welfare. He loved a good joke, and disliked "stuffed shirts" and formality. He and the first lady served hot dogs to the King and Queen of England at a Hyde Park picnic. F.D.R. liked baseball and enjoyed a game of poker with lots of wild cards. He wore a battered hat and old clothes on fishing trips, and everywhere he went he took a little black dog with him. He was warm and human.

By 1940, the war had begun in Europe. There was the danger that the United States might be attacked. It was election year, and Roosevelt had already served two terms. Reluctant to run again, he felt that he could not quit in a crisis and that he should undertake four more years of the presidential duties if the people wanted him. They got their chance to decide and, although many people were opposed to the idea of a third term, the majority chose Roosevelt again.

Feeling that his re-election meant that the people approved of his stand against the Axis, Roosevelt moved quickly to do everything short of war to help those who were still fighting the Axis. He procured the passage of the Lend-Lease Act, making food and munitions available to the Allies. He declared an unlimited national emergency to exist, and ordered our Navy to attack Axis submarines preying on our ships. Such things brought protests from the isolationists, but Roosevelt saw clearly that Hitler and the Japs were our mortal enemies.

In the Far East, we were facing the Japanese end of the Axis. Since we refused to abandon China, who had been fighting Japan for years, the Japs resolved to attack us too, and on December 7, 1941, the blow was struck at our fleet at Pearl Harbor. Four days later, Germany and Italy declared war against the United States. The die was cast. We joined the other countries that were fighting against the great evil that marched across the earth. We fought for our lives, and for a better world.

Under Roosevelt's leadership, the United Nations was formed to carry on the fight against the Axis and to plan to prevent future wars. Earlier, our crisis president had proclaimed America's desire for a world founded upon the Four Freedoms: freedom of speech, freedom of worship, freedom from want and freedom from fear.

Thenceforth, President Roosevelt devoted most of his time to the direction of our stupendous war effort. Conferring often with Prime Minister Churchill, he soon had the war plans of America and Britain fitted together and working as one. Complete teamwork with Soviet Russia was slower in coming, but much progress was made in 1943, when Roosevelt, Churchill and Stalin met at Teheran.

Early in 1945, following his election to a fourth term, Roosevelt met with the leaders of Great Britain and Russia, this time at Yalta. There the Big Three mapped out the final victory over Germany and laid plans for the peace to come. But the trip was strenuous and tiring. The strain had at last told on Franklin Roosevelt.

He went south to rest at Warm Springs. There on April 12th, he suffered a stroke and died a few hours later. Victory in Europe was only twenty-six days off and in the Pacific it came four months later, but the man who had given so much of himself to secure that victory was not to see it.

The sad news stunned people everywhere, in all the United Nations. Tribute poured in from all the world's leaders, outside the Axis. Americans in all walks of life, his opponents as well as his supporters, felt the shock and grieved. Men and women who had never seen him felt a sense of personal loss.

The historians tell us that we must wait to judge of Roosevelt's place in history. But, as Franklin D. Roosevelt was laid to rest in the garden of his beloved Hyde Park home, millions of people felt in their hearts that they had lost a friend, as well as a great leader. And they were determined that his carefully laid plans for a peaceful, happy world should be carried out. He would want that. That would be a fitting memorial.